HISTORIC HONG KONG

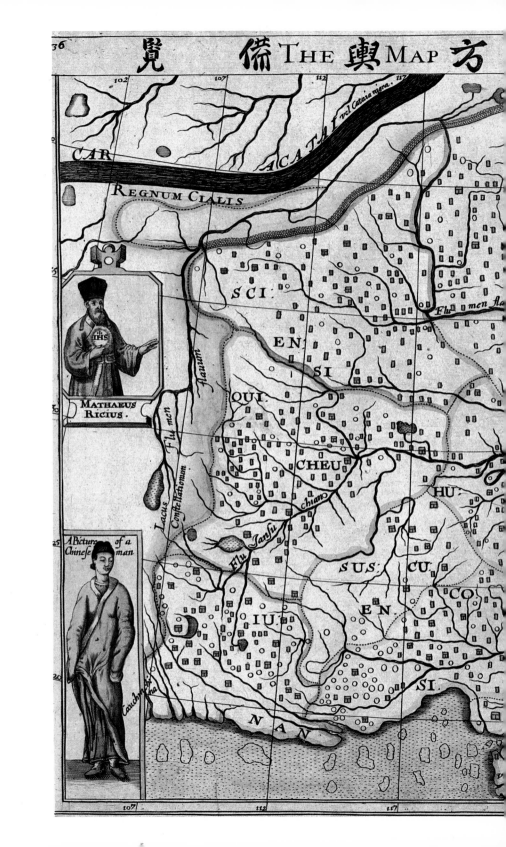

CAR

ACATAI vel Cataia nigra

REGNUM CIALIS

SCI

EN
SI

Flu men fla

QUI

Flaum

Lacus Conflictationum

Flu men

MATHAEUS RICIUS.

CHEU

HU

Iarsu chian

Iarsu

Flu

SUS

CU

CO

A Picture of a Chinese man

IU

EN

SI

Cauchinchina

NAN

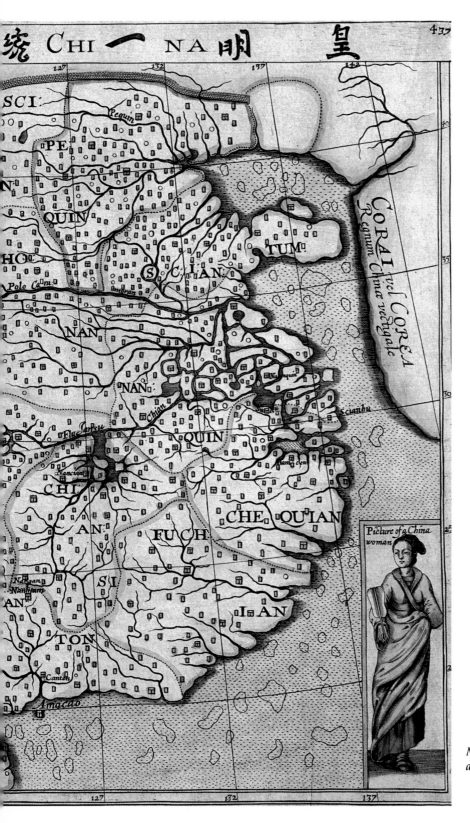

繞 CHI 一 NA 明 皇

SCI:

Pequin

PE

QUIN

HO

Polo Caim:

N

NAN

NAN

Chian

Flu Tansu

Nancian

QUIN

CHI

AN:

FUCH

SI:

N.Ngan:
Nanhum

AN

TON

Canton

Amacao

S CIAN

Andran

TUM

CORAI vel COREA
Regnum China vectigale

Nanquin

Scianhu

Pian ceu

CHE QUIAN

IAN

Picture of a China woman

Map of China, 1625, artist unknown

For Simon, Guy and Claire

HISTORIC HONG KONG

A VISITOR'S GUIDE

Sally Rodwell

ODYSSEY GUIDES
Hong Kong

Published by The Guidebook Company Limited in conjunction with the Hong Kong Tourist Association

Second Printing 1992

Project Editor: Mary McIntosh
Illustrations Editor: Caroline Robertson
Production Editor: Rose Borton
Design: Unity Design Studio
Map Artwork: Bai Yiliang
Index: Nick Wallwork

Front Cover: Postcard courtesy of Anne Selby
Illustrations supplied courtesy of: Altfield Gallery: 10, 23; Antiquities and Monuments Office: 18, 38 (top), 40, 43 (top right and middle), 44, 46 (bottom), 47 (bottom), 49, 68, 74, 86 (top), 90-91; Airphoto International: 140, 141, 160; Alan Birch: 135, 136, 137, 138, 139, 143; Alain Evrard: 144; David Chappell: 71, 146; The Chinese University, Hong Kong: 15, 19, 26, 27; Richard Dobson: 155; Government Information Service, Hong Kong: 34, 35 (top right), 38 (bottom), 42 (left and middle), 43 (bottom right), 46 (top), 53, 70, 125, 128-129; Karen Haney: 35 (bottom left), 47 (top), 73, 77, 116; Nigel Hicks: 120, 151, 152, 153, 156, 158; Heirlooms: 8, 12, 54; The Hongkong and Shanghai Bank 56, 61; Hong Kong Museum of Art: 2-3, 58, 80; Hong Kong Museum of History: 33, 39, 66, 82, 100, 123; William Meacham: map page 16; Public Records Office, Hong Kong: 63, 65, 75, 83, 86 (bottom), 93, 97, 99, 103, 105, 107, 112, 114, 122, 133, 134, 139; Brian Tilbrook 76, 111

Produced by Twin Age Ltd, Hong Kong

ISBN 962-217-212-1
Printed in Hong Kong
Cover: Queen's Road Central as it used to be in the early 1900s

Sally Rodwell obtained her first degree in Chinese, Archaeology and Anthropology at Lucy Cavendish College, University of Cambridge; she gained an M Phil in East Asian Archaeology, also at Cambridge, in 1984. During her studies she spent a year in China with her family from 1979 to 1980.

Married with two children, Sally Rodwell lived in Hong Kong in the mid-1970s and again from 1985 to 1990, serving as a member of the Hong Kong Government's Antiquities Advisory Board for four years until 1990.

An early photo taken from The Peak, Hong Kong Island.
The Kowloon Peninsula is clearly visible, with the mountains
of the New Territories in the distance

Acknowledgements

Douglas King of the Hong Kong Tourist Association commissioned this book and has given unfailing support to the project. I am grateful to Carl Smith for reading the manuscript and for his helpful criticism and advice.

I would like to thank Melinda Welker, Edward Hepting and Asa Chan, also from the Hong Kong Tourist Association, for help with sourcing materials, as well as the Antiquities and Monuments Office, particularly Alex Yip Cho-hong, Tom Ming Kay-chuen and Fung Chung-shek. Thanks are due to Sally Stewart, Anthony Tsui and Piers Gray at the University of Hong Kong; my sister-in-law, Gill Townsend; my brother, William Clark of the Royal Engineers; Harry Wilken of Central Registration and Ian Ward of the Royal Hong Kong Police; May Hung of Jardine Pacific Ltd; Stella See of the Tung Wah Group of Hospitals; Joffre Chan at the Museum of History; Sarah Tsui of the Public Records Office; G F Da Silva of the Urban Services Department; and Sonia Wilhelm of the Jewish Historical Society. Bill Greaves of the Architectural Services Department contributed to the list of place names.

I am grateful to Magnus Bartlett and Geoff Cloke of The Guidebook Company for taking on the task of publishing the book. Mary McIntosh has edited the manuscript superbly and I must thank Rose Borton, Caroline Robertson and George Ngan for their contributions to the project.

Above all thanks are due to my husband, Simon, for his constructive criticism and for accompanying me on numerous expeditions to out-of-the-way places in Hong Kong during the past five years.

A view of Hong Kong harbour by T Allom, 1843

PREFACE

In 1841 Lord Palmerston dismissed Hong Kong as 'a barren island with hardly a house upon it'. His remark has led many people to believe that the Hong Kong region was largely uninhabited before the arrival of the British.

In fact nothing could be further from the truth. Archaeologists have found evidence of human habitation, both on the Island and in the New Territories, from as early as 4,000 BC; and the archaeological and historical record of the various people who have lived here now has very few gaps.

The purpose of this book is to look at the common heritage of the Hong Kong people, both ancient and recent, which can still be found in the region. Despite relentless and unceasing development—and redevelopment—in Hong Kong and the New Territories, clusters of old buildings, fortifications and monuments remain. These illuminate the dry historical record and remind us in our daily lives of Hong Kong's varied, rich and dynamic past.

The buildings and monuments discussed are mainly gazetted monuments and those graded by the Antiquities Advisory Board, but I have also included some that are in private hands. I have used the customary local romanisation of Cantonese names for people and places in Hong Kong; as far as possible, I have used *pinyin* for names of Chinese people and places in the People's Republic of China. Exceptions include the usual English renderings of Canton and Peking.

I hope readers will have as much pleasure discovering parts of old Hong Kong as I have had in writing this brief guide.

Sally Rodwell
Hong Kong
March 1990

Parade near St John's Cathedral, *woodblock engraving
published in* The Illustrated London News, *1857*

CONTENTS

PREHISTORY
HONG KONG'S EARLIEST INHABITANTS

The story of human habitation in the territory of Hong Kong begins at the end of the last Ice Age (15,000 - 8,000 BC) when the northern glaciers began to melt. The sea level rose in many parts of the world and the Hong Kong region, once an inland, mountainous area, was gradually surrounded by the rising seas.

During the coldest part of the Ice Age the sea level was 80 - 100 metres lower than it is today and Hong Kong was located far to the west of the South China Sea. Probably at that time people lived in sheltered lowland valleys, or by the seashore on the wide continental shelf. However, this land has been submerged for the past 6,000 years and so far no evidence of Ice Age, or pre-Ice Age, occupation by man has been found.

With the gradual warming of the climate and the rising seas, early settlers would have been forced repeatedly to move inland to higher ground until the coastline finally stabilised at its present level around 4,000 BC. Shells from the lowest levels of the archaeological site at Sham Wan on Lamma Island have been radiocarbon-dated to 4,400 BC, indicating that by that time the sea level was only two metres below where it is today.

All of Hong Kong's 12 earliest habitation sites are located on sand bars above the beach, except for one at Sai Wan on Cheung Chau, which is on a low ridge overlooking the sea. On Hong Kong Island only one prehistoric site, at Chung Hom Wan, has been excavated so far.

No remains of any buildings or structures have been found at any of Hong Kong's prehistoric sites, although buildings made of wood or bamboo would have decayed fairly rapidly in the acidic soil, leached by torrential rain. What is usually found at habitation sites is food débris (bones of pigs, deer, marine catfish, sharks, rays and dolphins), stone tools and pottery. We can speculate that the people led a seafaring life, moving around the coast in boats, embarking on fishing expeditions and also possibly experimenting with agriculture.

From the early period of Hong Kong's Stone Age two types of low-fired pottery have been found: coarse sandy ware with stamped cord impressions and fine, incised paste; and then later 'geometric' grey ware with net, herringbone and trellis designs, fired at more than 1,000°C. Stone tools include axes, adzes (for woodworking), slotted rings and other ornaments, grinding stones and chipped pebble tools. Later types of polished stone artefacts include daggers, flanged stone rings, knives and projectile points.

Later Stone Age sites include Shek Pik on Lantau, Tai Kwai Wan on Cheung Chau, and Sham Wan and Lo So Sing on Lamma Island.

The Bronze Age in Hong Kong is marked by the appearance of bronze implements in archaeological deposits dating from about 1,200 BC. It is not clear whether knowledge of bronze-working was transmitted from early bronze-working cultures in the Yangtze Basin, in Yunnan Province or in North Vietnam; nor is it certain whether it was linked to the spread of increased social differentiation, writing, kingship or organised religion. We know very little about the political and social organisation of the Bronze Age people.

Bronze Age artefacts which have been excavated locally include fish-hooks, projectile points, knives and axe-heads. Moulds for making vessels, bells and hairpins have also been found. In the Bronze Age 'geometric' pottery was fired at a higher temperature, making it much harder, and decoration included new circle, spiral and 'double-F' designs. Vessels were thrown on a wheel and glazes started to be used.

Bronze Age burial sites as well as habitation sites have been found on Lantau at Man Kok Tsui, Shek Pik and Hai Dei Wan, and at Tai Wan on Lamma. However, no permanent habitation sites or structures have been discovered in Hong Kong, leading us to the assumption that the people retained their shifting way of life, much of which may have been spent in boats.

An intriguing insight into the Bronze Age in Hong Kong

(above) Axe heads and weapons dating from the Bronze Age; (below) Neolithic coarse-corded cooking pot, Lantau Island

15

is provided by rock carvings discovered in remote parts of the territory. Located at Shek Pik, Tung Lung Island, Po Toi Island, Big Wave Bay and Wong Chuk Hang on Hong Kong Island, Cheung Chau and Kau Sai Chau, these carvings are similar in design to those found on local Bronze Age artefacts. Rock paintings and carvings in other parts of the world usually have some sort of ritual or religious significance. We do not know the significance of these carvings, but most of them are located close to the sea on rocky outcrops and they were evidently of importance to the local people.

Much of our knowledge about Bronze Age people in Hong Kong and on the South China coast comes from accounts written by later Chinese historians. They generally referred to the southerners as barbarians, but the local people called themselves the Yueh. It is thought that the Yueh comprised many separate tribes with different languages and customs which varied from region to region along the South China coast. The Han historian, Si-ma Qian (145 - c 90 BC), described the inhabitants of Min Yueh as 'cutting the hair short, tattooing the body, possessing neither towns nor villages but living in valleys of bamboo, expert at fighting on the water but of no use on land, having neither chariots nor horses nor bows and arrows'. In terms of their way of life, Hong Kong's Bronze Age people may well have been the predecessors of the present-day Tanka and Hoklo fishing families who live in Hong Kong waters.

Estimated coastline (solid line) around 10000 BC in the Hong Kong area, from Archaeology in Hong Kong *by William Meacham (1980)*

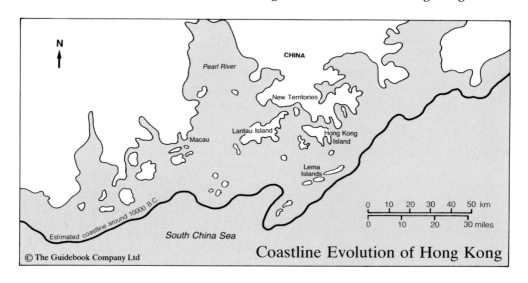

PREHISTORIC SITES AND ROCK CARVINGS

Shek Pik

Shek Pik, with remains from the late Stone Age and the Bronze Age, is one of the most interesting prehistoric sites in Hong Kong. It was discovered and excavated by Walter Schofield in 1937.

Schofield had discovered more than 100 sites in the Hong Kong region between 1933 and 1936, but his excavation at Tung Wan (the eastern part of the beach at Shek Pik) was the only site in Hong Kong where complete burials accompanied by funerary objects were found. It proved that in certain favourable conditions in Hong Kong, human and animal bones could survive from prehistoric times. All six burials were oriented with the head to the south. Perhaps this was an early expression of *feng shui* geomantic beliefs.

Most of the funerary objects were lost during World War II but, fortunately, Schofield had already given some of the stone adzes and bronzes to the British Museum. His detailed site report has been of immense value to prehistorians.

Schofield concluded that the Hong Kong area was a meeting-place of cultures and probably also of races; it had trading relations with other lands, and formed part of a cultural province extending a considerable distance along the China coast. During the past 50 years Schofield's views have been borne out by further excavations in Hong Kong and extensive excavations in China.

Between 1938 and 1941, exploration of prehistoric remains at Shek Pik was conducted by a scholar named Chen Kung-chieh. The artefacts from his excavations have also been lost, except for a few which came to light in 1972. A member of the Archaeological Society who worked for the Hongkong and Shanghai Bank was told that a trunk containing old vessels had been found in one of the Bank's warehouses. The torn label on the trunk bore the characters 'Kung' and 'Chieh'. When the artefacts were compared with photographs of finds in Chen's Shek Pik site report it was concluded that the artefacts were probably those from the excavation.

17

The site was excavated again in 1979 by R J Frost but this time finds were few and fragmentary. Undeterred, in 1987 a fourth archaeologist, Au Ga Fat, excavated the site once more, accompanied by archaeologists from Guangdong and the Chinese University of Hong Kong. Although he found few artefacts, he made what may have been two very important discoveries of a rather different nature.

140 centimetres below the surface of the sand bar Au found what appeared to be seven post-holes, spaced at regular intervals, forming two lines at an angle of 90° to each other. Au excavated the holes and photographed them, but he had hardly completed the task when the weather broke and several days of heavy rain caused the walls of the pit to collapse. Everything was drowned in tons of sand. However, if these were indeed post-holes they would be the earliest evidence of structures from the Stone Age to be found in Hong Kong.

Having exhausted his funds on the first phase of this excavation, but feeling that the site could still yield important data, Au was determined to press on. He recruited prisoners from the nearby detention centre at Shek Pik and they excavated very large areas of the beach. Au's second find, possibly of great importance, was what he thought may have been the remains of a kiln. Without doubt Shek Pik will continue to interest prehistorians in years to come.

Rock Carvings at Shek Pik

The rock carvings at Shek Pik were discovered by Chen Kung-chieh in 1939. The local villagers drew his attention to an engraved rock on the upper part of the beach to the west of Tung Wan. They told him there had been a second rock carving on the opposite side of the valley but the rock, split in half by lightning, now lay face down so the design could not be seen.

However, the villagers were insistent that there was a third carving further up the valley. Eventually, in 1962, a carving was discovered on a steep slope two kilometres away.

The lower Shek Pik carving is thought to date from the Bronze Age, and similar carvings can be found at Cheung Chau, Po Toi, Big Wave Bay, Kau Sai Chau, Lung Ha Wan, Wong Chuk Hang and Tung Lung. Most of the carvings are geometric, spiral designs, some with stylised animal faces

Rock carving at Wong Chuk Hang, near Aberdeen (left above); rock carving at Shek Pik beach, Lantau (left below), Bronze Age.
Three prehistoric stone drills 4000– 1200 BC (top); a neolithic jade bird pendant, 3500 BC (bottom)

embodied in the pattern, similar to designs on local Bronze Age pottery. The purpose of the carvings is not known, but it is thought that they must have had some religious significance for the local people.

The upper Shek Pik carving, which is less accessible, has a 'games board' grid design. Similar carvings have been found at Tung Chung, Ting Kok Village and on Hoi Ha Beach. These carvings may well be graffiti from a much later period and are probably not connected with the earlier ones.

Sham Wan

Located at the southern end of Lamma Island, Sham Wan is a long walk from the ferries at either Sok Kwu Wan or Yung Shue Wan. The easiest way to reach the high sand bar site is by boat. Although Walter Schofield and other archaeologists knew that Sham Wan was a prehistoric site from observation of surface finds, the sand bar was not investigated scientifically until its 'rediscovery' by William Meacham in 1971.

As a result of excavations carried out between 1971 and 1977, archaeologists were able to establish an accurate chronology and cultural sequence for the entire region. The location of the pits can still be distinguished today.

Dr Solomon Bard directed excavations during three of the five seasons of digging. He was accompanied by specialists from many other disciplines, who produced scientific reports on the different types of finds.

The sequence of layers spanned 6,000 years, right back to the Stone Age, and each period of Hong Kong's prehistory was represented, making Sham Wan one of Hong Kong's most important archaeological sites. The depth of cultural deposits extended to 3.3 metres.

The upper layers were dated by coins and pottery from the historical periods while, for the first time in Hong Kong, samples from the prehistoric layers were dated by the radiocarbon and thermoluminescence methods.

The scientific methods of excavation and analysis of finds at Sham Wan represented a major step forward in Hong Kong archaeology.

Rock Carving at Wong Chuk Hang

Of all the rock carvings in Hong Kong, the Bronze Age carving at Wong Chuk Hang is exceptional in that it is located 1.5 kilometres from the sea. Engraved on a vertical rock face in three groups, it is composed of flowing spiral designs and perceptible animal faces. The carving is similar to those on Cheung Chau and Po Toi. It was reported by local residents to the Antiquities and Monuments Office in 1983.

Rock Carving on Tung Lung Island

The Tung Lung carving was first recorded in 1819 in the Chinese Qing Dynasty San On County gazetteer. Located on a large rock four metres above sea level, it is the largest rock carving in Hong Kong, with a height of 180 centimetres and a width at the base of 240 centimetres. Some say the right-hand part of the carving depicts a bird, while others consider the entire engraving resembles a dragon. Apart from this rock carving Tung Lung has no known prehistoric sites.

CONQUEST BY THE CHINESE
FROM THE HAN TO THE QING DYNASTY

 In 214 BC the army of Qin Shi Huang-di, the Qin emperor, conquered the Yueh people and the Hong Kong region became part of the first Chinese empire. For administrative purposes the region was divided into prefectures which were further subdivided into counties.

Although the northern Chinese maintained direct rule from Canton to west of Hainan Island, they did not colonise the area. Instead they built fortified cities, occupied by soldiers and traders, and left the local Yueh people to carry on their lives much as before.

When the dynasty fell in 210 BC, the governor of Nan-hai Prefecture (which included the Hong Kong region), set up an independent kingdom. The area was ruled by his descendants, who continued to send tribute to the northern capital until they were conquered by the Han emperor's armies in 111 BC.

The Hong Kong region remained part of Pan-yu County in Nan-hai Prefecture until AD 331 when it came under the administration of Bao-an County. The name of the area was altered again in 757 when it became part of Dongguan.

During the Tang Dynasty (618 - 907), Canton and the other southern Chinese garrisons were occupied by soldiers, exiles and foreign traders — Jews, Christians and Muslims. Imports included ivory, frankincense, copper ingots, turtle shells and rhinoceros horns; silk and porcelain were exported. And from Canton foreign ships carried Chinese Buddhists on pilgrimages to India.

Although the valleys in Hong Kong were not yet being cultivated intensively, we know that salt and lime were produced locally. Salt was taxed, and villages that later had extensive salt-fields have names that reflect the economic activity there, such as Yim Tin Tsai in Tolo Harbour and

Yim Tin at Tai O — *yim tin* is Cantonese for 'salt-field'.

Today many remains of Tang Dynasty lime-kilns can be found in Hong Kong. Lime was used as a cleansing agent, as a fertiliser, as a component of whitewash and cement, and for careening boats.

Although it has been completely redeveloped in recent years, Tuen Mun in the New Territories has the distinction of being the first place in Hong Kong to which there are historical references. An itinerary published in the Tang official history notes: 'From Canton travelling towards the southeast for 200 miles you reach Mount Tuen Mun.' It also records the presence of a garrison there.

Guarding the mouth of the Pearl River, Tuen Mun with its excellent harbour was the first port of call for ships travelling from Canton to Southeast Asia and beyond. As in prehistoric times, the Hong Kong region was very much an international crossroads.

Two Tang scholars, Han Yu and Liu Yu-xi, mentioned Tuen Mun in their poems. Han Yu, passing through the area on his way to exile in Chao-zhou, is reputed to have

Line engraving of Hong Kong harbour by T Allom, 1843

engraved the characters *kao shan dai yat* ('high mountain first in merit') on a tablet at Castle Peak monastery at Tuen Mun. Others claim that the tablet was actually inscribed later by a Song scholar, Tang Fuxie, in memory of Han Yu.

With the fall of the Tang Dynasty at the beginning of the tenth century and the establishment of the southern state of Nan Han by King Liu, the garrison at Tuen Mun was strengthened and a naval force was based at Tuen Mun to maintain order along the coast.

King Liu, a passionate lover of pearls, also established an organisation to exploit the pearl-producing areas off the South China coast. Of these, Tolo Harbour in the New Territories was renowned for its pearl-bearing oysters. Here many local fishermen worked as pearl fishers; although the work was dangerous it was well paid. The Nan Han kings adorned their palaces with pearls and exploited the oyster beds for all they were worth.

When the Song army conquered the area in the second half of the tenth century, the new emperor was persuaded that intensive pearl fishing was harmful to the local people. He issued an edict forbidding people from making their living from pearl fishing. The ban remained in force until it was lifted in 1114 and officials were once more appointed to obtain tribute paid in pearls.

In succeeding dynasties state intervention in the gathering of pearls was intermittent, with frequent over-exploitation by both the government and individuals. By the end of the 17th century the oyster beds were almost exhausted and large-scale pearl fishing was abandoned.

In the Song Dynasty (960 – 1279) the naval arm of the garrison at Tuen Mun was expanded in order to police inshore waters against raids by pirates and bandits. The town impressed the Song poet, Jiang Zhi-chi, who visited Tuen Mun and mentioned it in his poems.

Before the Song Dynasty there are no records of any land tenure, but during this period Cantonese-speaking farmers from further north gradually began to settle in the region and they cultivated the fertile river-valleys.

From the genealogy of the Tang clan at Kam Tin in the New Territories we know that in the 11th century the founding ancestor, Tang Fuxie, was a member of the gentry, a *jinshi* scholar from Jiangxi. After serving as a magistrate in Guangdong and being enchanted by the local climate

24

and scenery, he decided to retire in the area. He acquired land in Kam Tin, founded the village and built a college.

The Tang family prospered and younger members of the clan owned lands in Dong-guan and as far north as Jiangxi Province, as well as throughout the New Territories and on Lantau to the south.

When the emperor's family was captured in 1127 after being driven out of the Song capital, Kaifeng, by the Mongols, one princess managed to escape and she sought refuge with the Tangs in Jiangxi, where Tang Xian was district magistrate. The Tangs sent her to their family seat at Kam Tin in the New Territories where she married the magistrate's son, Tang Sze-ming. When her father defeated the Mongols and became emperor he recognised his daughter's marriage and gave her husband a title and a large dowry.

The Tang clan is the largest of the five great clans of the New Territories. The genealogy of the Hau clan, originally from Canton, also goes back to the 11th century. The Pangs came from Jiangxi in the late Song Dynasty; the Lius arrived in the 14th century and the Mans arrived shortly afterwards.

The incoming Cantonese were eventually called Punti (meaning 'from this native land') and they are descendants of people from North China who migrated south.

The Tanka and the Hoklo, possibly the descendants of the prehistoric Yueh tribes, are thought to have inhabited the South China coast from time immemorial. They are primarily seafarers and fishermen who live in boats and make temporary settlements along the shore, such as the stilt village at Tai O on Lantau. The Hoklo probably originated from Fujian Province to the northeast. Although the two groups continue to live and work in Hong Kong waters, they do not intermarry and to this day they have different customs.

The end of the Song Dynasty was an exciting period for Hong Kong. Legend has it that the two Song boy emperors and their mothers made their home in the area while Chinese forces attempted in vain to repel the conquering Mongols.

In 1276, fleeing from the Mongol invaders, the court travelled south to Fuzhou in Fujian Province. The princes' elder brother, Emperor Gong-di, had already surrendered to the Mongols and the hopes of the Chinese people rested with the two little princes. At the age of nine Di Zheng, the elder of the two, was declared emperor.

However, the Mongol armies continued to fight their way southwards and towards the end of 1276 the imperial entourage was forced to travel by boat to Guangdong to seek refuge and make a new base. The following year Di Zheng established his travelling court at Mui Wo (Silvermine Bay) on Lantau, moving two months later to Guan-fu Chang in the area of the present Kowloon City.

Here there was an established naval outpost as well as a resident Song official responsible for supervision of taxation of the salt industry. A fine travelling palace was built, together with a lookout on a hill overlooking Kowloon Bay. It is thought that the Sung Wong Toi rock carving dates from the six-month stay of the boy emperor and his court.

During 1277 the Song armies had a few military successes and they managed to regain several cities from the Mongols. The Mongols, however, renewed their attack on southern China and organised a combined onslaught by land and sea on Di Zheng's Kowloon headquarters. The emperor and his brother retreated to Tsuen Wan and then to Humen further up the Pearl River estuary, harassed by the Mongol fleet, eventually crossing the estuary into Heung Shan.

The following year the Song forces regained Canton and Di Zheng, by then seriously ill, moved back to Lantau. He died there at the age of 11 and was succeeded as emperor by his brother, Di Bing, aged seven. The court only stayed on Lantau for about three months before moving on to Yaishan in China. Here in 1279, with their backs to the sea, they were caught between the Mongol forces on the land and the Mongol fleet offshore. It is thought that in the confusion Di Bing, carried in the arms of one of his officials, was drowned at sea.

During the succeeding Yuan Dynasty (1276 - 1368) coastal trade declined and the garrison at Tuen Mun was scaled down. The Ming Dynasty (1368 – 1644) saw the reorganisation of military bases and Tuen Mun's role as a garrison was taken over by Nantou, situated a few miles further along the Pearl River estuary, at a location which commanded the passage of all deep-water vessels to Canton.

In the 15th and 16th centuries the coastal communities of Guangdong Province were continually harassed by

A Tang Dynasty tomb cover, AD 672 (top); a neolithic cloud-shaped ornament made of jade, 3500 BC (bottom)

26

Japanese pirates who would take advantage of the prevailing winds in the summer months and sail to Guangdong on raiding expeditions. Chinese officials decided the only way to combat the problem was to establish a maritime defence force. A network of forts and outposts was built at strategic locations along the coast to deter the Japanese marauders, and patrols were carried out by Chinese war junks.

The waters of the Pearl River estuary are very shallow between Macau and Canton. The only navigable channels lie either side of Lantau Island, close to the Nantou Peninsula — hence the strategic significance of Nantou, 'the gateway to Canton', and the location of forts at Fan Lau on the southern tip and Tung Chung on the west coast of Lantau; at Tung Lung to the east of Hong Kong Island; and at Tuen Mun.

Besides pirates, in the 16th century the Chinese faced another threat — the Portuguese. In 1514 Portuguese traders made their base at Tuen Mun, erecting fortifications and manufacturing ammunition. They were followed in 1517 by an envoy named Thomas Pirez, sent by the Portuguese governor at Malacca with a convoy of four ships to call on the Viceroy at Canton and then make his way north to the capital, Peking. Pirez's visit marks the beginning of diplomatic relations between Portugal and China.

However, while the ships were in Canton, disease broke out amongst the Portuguese and all except Pirez retreated to Tuen Mun. Here the Portuguese, led by Simão d'Andrade, angered local Chinese officials by refusing to pay customs duties, by robbing local inhabitants and by executing prisoners. Eventually, in 1521, the Chinese sent a force to quell the Portuguese and it soundly beat them. The Portuguese withdrew and subsequently concentrated their efforts on the establishment of a base at Macau, where Chinese officials felt they could be safely contained at arm's length from Canton.

In 1573 the administration of Dongguan County (of which Hong Kong was a part) was reorganised and a new county was formed, comprising the region immediately surrounding Nantou and including Hong Kong. It was called Xin-an (San On in Cantonese). Surviving county gazetteers — local government records — provide a wealth of information about the history of each area.

We learn from the gazetteers that the problem of Japanese

A Tang funeral urn excavated in the Guangzhou region, c AD 618 - 907

27

pirates worsened towards the end of the Ming Dynasty. For the new Qing administration the arrival of yet more Europeans wishing to trade also presented difficulties. However, the officials' worst nightmare was the possibility of attack from the sea by the Ming rebel leader, Zheng Cheng-gong (known in the West as Koxinga), who was based in Taiwan.

Finally, in 1662, they took action. The Viceroy and the Governor of Guangdong Province jointly gave the order that a strip of land 50 *li* (27 kilometres) wide, bordering the coast, should be evacuated and all the inhabitants moved inland. In this way the pirates and rebels could not obtain food and provisions from the local people. Rebellion and piracy in coastal waters would be eliminated simultaneously.

As it turned out, the evacuation caused the people of Hong Kong great suffering. They lost their lands and many houses were demolished to provide materials for fortifications in the coastal strip. Deprived of their livelihood, many of the uprooted villagers starved and died. And because the coastal villages were unoccupied, the pirates were able to obtain a foothold in the region.

After several years, realising that the 'scorched earth' policy had been a failure, the Governor of Guangdong lifted the evacuation order and the depleted coastal population was allowed to return home. Immigration was also encouraged in an effort to revitalise the region, which was now providing little revenue from agriculture and salt production.

Hakka people from the north moved into the area, in some cases occupying Punti villages, but usually farming the higher, less fertile lands. Known as 'guest people', the Hakkas with their own language and customs, were northern Chinese who had been forced out of their lands in the Central Plains.

Although from time to time there was friction between the Punti and the Hakkas, for the most part the two groups lived side by side fairly peacefully. The 1819 edition of the San On gazetteer records that in the region that was later to come under British rule there were 455 Punti and 225 Hakka villages. By the time the British arrived in 1840 Hong Kong Island, although originally owned by the Punti Tang clan, was almost entirely occupied by Hakkas.

Despite the resettlement of the coastal region in 1669, the problems caused by pirates in Hong Kong waters were far from solved. Many pirates were Chinese rebels, outlaws who hated the new Manchu regime.

The most famous pirate was Zhang Baozi (Cheung Po-tsai in Cantonese). He was the son of a fisherman in Guangdong Province who, at the age of 15, was carried off by the pirate king, Cheng Yat, to live the life of an outlaw.

In 1808 Cheng Yat's ship foundered in a storm near Indonesia and he was drowned. His wife assumed command of his fleet and she fell in love with the young Cheung Po-tsai. Cheung swiftly rose to power, and he was given command of a division of the robber fleet. He soon made a name for himself as a man of integrity, treating his followers fairly and refraining from exploitation of the villagers from whom he bought provisions.

Cheung's fleet numbered more than 270 ships and 30,000 men. Foreign merchants calling at Canton would pay the pirates protection money in order to avoid danger and loss. Pirate hideouts and camps were built at Tung Chung on Lantau, and at Sai Ying Pun and Quarry Bay on Hong Kong Island. Cheung Po-tsai is said to have built Man Mo Temple in Hollywood Road and a fort half way up Mount Gough, between May Road and Kotewall Road, while the Tin Hau temples at Ma Wan, Cheung Chau and Chek Chue (Stanley) were apparently used as outposts.

Cheung's ultimate ambition — to overthrow the ruling Qing Dynasty — was frustrated by the able mandarin, Pai Ling, the Viceroy of the Two Guangs (Guangdong and Guangxi provinces). He decided to allow the people who lived by the sea to form their own militia and to cast their own cannon for use in self-defence.

Pai Ling forbade villagers in the coastal region from supplying pirates with provisions, and he banned Chinese merchant ships from sailing in pirate-infested waters. Salt was to be transported overland instead.

Pai Ling's measures were effective. The pirates ran short of food and increased their attacks on foreign shipping. The Portuguese armed their ships and patrolled the approaches to Macau, but they were still preyed upon by the pirates. Eventually the East India Company offered to help the Chinese authorities and the Portuguese followed suit. The pirates were then faced with the combined opposition of the Chinese Government and the foreign merchants. Anxious to restore law and order, Pai Ling decided to grant the pirates an amnesty if they ceased their activities, the only alternative being annihilation.

The final showdown took place at Chek Lap Kok off the west coast of Lantau in 1810. Cheung Po-tsai and the wife of Cheng Yat were surrounded by Chinese, English and Macanese ships. They appealed for help from their fellow pirate chief, Kuo Po-tai, but Kuo was a jealous rival and he left them to their fate. Cheung, however, managed to fight his way out of the blockade and, once free, was poised to take revenge against Kuo. Knowing he could expect no mercy, Kuo surrendered to the Qing authorities and was rewarded with an official post. Seeing Kuo safely ensconced in the government administration, Cheung realised the authorities would keep their word so he and Cheng Yat's wife decided to surrender.

The pirates' petition of surrender to Pai Ling was eloquent:

We were your good subjects once, but for a number of reasons, we became pirates. At first, there was only a small group of us. The dearth of recent years has helped to increase the number, and we have been forced to rob and pillage in order to live. Hence we have become offenders against the law. As pirates, we live far away from our home. We have no family life. The feeling of despondency increases. We have to struggle with the wind and waves. Our condition is pitiable and we beg you to grant us our lives. We understand that you, the Governor-general, are kind and understanding, and you love your people as your sons. Even a bird wishes to return to its nest; a fish cannot find comfort in boiling water. We wish to express our sincerity by this petition signed by the division. We hope that you will pity us and save us from fire and water; forgive us our offence and open for us a new way of life. We solemnly promise to put an end to our career as pirates and to devote our time to farming. We are looking forward to the day when we may praise you in song.

Although Cheung's surrender was welcomed by the authorities, other pirates refused to give in. Being familiar with their hide-outs, Cheung offered to go and capture them and put an end to piracy in the region. Pai Ling reluctantly agreed, on condition that Cheng Yat's wife, and

30

wives of the pirates who accompanied him, should remain in Canton as hostages. Cheung consented to this and accomplished his mission with honour. The ensuing peace was commemorated by naming the Peak on Hong Kong Island Tai Ping Shan (Pacific Peak), and many of the reformed pirates may have continued to live at the foot of the mountain, in Sai Ying Pun.

The origin of the name Hong Kong relates to the production of incense in the region. *Hong* means 'fragrant', or 'incense', and *kong* means 'harbour'. The romanisation is a rendering of the Tanka boat people's pronunciation.

Introduced from North Vietnam, the incense tree, *Aquilaria sinensis*, flourished in the soils around Hong Kong. The wood was collected from growers throughout the region, assembled at Tsim Sha Tsui and shipped in junks to Shek Pai Wan (Aberdeen) on Hong Kong Island, where it was loaded into large vessels sailing in and out of Canton.

Although it has now died out, the industry reached the height of its prosperity in the Ming Dynasty. Huge quantities of incense continue to be burnt at most festivals in the Chinese calendar. Incense from Hong Kong was used in cities as far away as Suzhou, hundreds of miles to the north.

Hong Kong is an alternative name for the bay, Shek Pai Wan, situated in Aberdeen Harbour. There was once a small village at the eastern end of the bay called Hong Kong Village and this village used to act as the sole export agent for a special variety of incense that was highly valued.

It is generally thought that the first British seamen who landed on the island at Aberdeen named it Hong Kong in error, perhaps on being told by the local boat people the name of what they considered to be the most important harbour.

As we shall see in the next chapter, the settlement of Hong Kong Island by the British in 1841 was to have a dramatic effect on the lives of the scattered fishing and farming communities of Hong Kong.

MONUMENTS FROM THE HAN TO THE QING DYNASTY

Han Tomb, Lei Cheng Uk

The Han tomb at Lei Cheng Uk in Sham Shui Po, Kowloon, nearly 2,000 years old, was discovered in August 1955 by workmen levelling a hill in a squatter area in preparation for the construction of a resettlement estate. It was subsequently excavated by a team from the University of Hong Kong under the direction of Professor F S Drake.

On completion of the excavation the outer part of the tomb was cased in a concrete shell to prevent further deterioration. The tomb was opened to the public in June 1957, together with a small museum nearby housing finds from the site.

Made of brick with four barrel-vaulted chambers, the tomb was built in the form of a cross. The central chamber, linking the four arms of the cruciform, has a domed roof constructed by laying the bricks in a spiral. No mortar was used but soft red pottery tiles fill the gaps in the vaulting. The floor is also of bricks.

It is thought that the Lei Cheng Uk tomb dates from the middle of the Eastern Han Dynasty, that is, from the end of the first century AD to the middle of the second century. There are numerous stamped inscriptions and patterns on the bricks. The inscriptions, repeated in several places, read: 'Great fortune to Pan-yu', 'Peace to Pan-yu' and 'Master Xue'. During the Eastern Han period (23 BC – AD 220) Kowloon was part of Pan-yu County. Perhaps Master Xue was the brickmaker.

Although 58 bronze and pottery objects were found in the tomb, there was no body. Probably grave-robbers entered the tomb in the intervening centuries, desecrating the body and removing any valuables.

As in similar tombs of the period, the objects placed in the tomb were intended for use by the deceased in the afterlife. The pottery represents objects used by Chinese people of the Eastern Han period in their daily lives. These include models of houses, granaries, wells and stoves together with vessels for food, wine and cooking, and

32

The Han Tomb, Lei Cheng Uk (above); pottery model house (bottom left);
Ding *(tripod) with cover, green-glazed (bottom right);*
Han Dynasty AD 24-220, Lei Cheng Uk

Castle Peak Monastery, near Tuen Mun

storage jars. The few bronze objects, all in fragments, include a mirror, some bowls and a bell.

Probably the tomb at Lei Cheng Uk was built for a Chinese officer attached to a local garrison. It is one of a number of Han tombs found in the Pearl River delta in recent years, the nearest to Hong Kong being a group at Nantou in Shenzhen.

Tang Lime-kilns

Lime was made by burning coral and seashells in kilns, usually near the seashore. It was used in cement, as whitewash, for fertilising the fields and for cleaning the hulls of junks. The industry seems to have died out in this area by AD 1,000, only to reappear in the 18th and 19th centuries.

There are clusters of lime-kilns dating from the Tang Dynasty (618 – 907) in many parts of Hong Kong, the greatest number being found at Lo So Shing on Lamma, Yi Long Wan on Lantau and Tai Kwai Wan on Cheung Chau. Yi Long Wan is one of the best places to see these very early lime-kilns. In front of the Sea Ranch estate three kilns have been protected for display. Originally they had domed roofs, but none has survived intact.

Castle Peak Monastery

Castle Peak was first known as Bei Du Shan, named after the Buddhist saint, Bei Du, who founded a monastery on its slopes in the Liu Song Dynasty (AD 420 – 479). According to legend Bei Du was a roguish, vagabond monk who was able to cross rivers miraculously in a small wooden bowl. His name means 'cup ferry'.

Legend has it that Bei Du once stole a gold statue of the Buddha from his host after spending the night in his house. He was pursued by men on horseback who could not catch up with him even though he was travelling on foot. Finally they cornered Bei Du at a river but he escaped by crossing it in his wooden bowl, still clutching the gold statue.

Also known locally as Tsing Shan ('Green Mountain'), Bei Du Shan was designated a sacred mountain by Imperial Decree in 969, and it is mentioned many times in Chinese records.

The monastery at Castle Peak has been rebuilt several times during the past 1,500 years. The existing monastery,

36

perched on several terraces high on the hill overlooking Tuen Mun and surrounded by groves of bamboo, dates only from 1918 but it is rustic, beautiful and unspoiled.

More interesting perhaps than the monastery itself is the roughly-hewn, granite statue of Bei Du, thought to have been commissioned in 954 by an officer in the nearby garrison. It sits in a cave located behind and above the monastery.

Next to the cave is a replica of an inscription carved on a rock at the top of the mountain, reputedly by the Tang scholar, Han Yu, or perhaps later by a founding member of the New Territories Tang clan. It reads *kao shan dai yat* — 'high mountain, first in merit'. However, the exact location of the original inscription mentioned in Chinese records is no longer known.

The ancient rocks of Castle Peak are full of fossils. There is another small cave near the Bei Du statue where the fossil of what appears to be a giant vertebra, nearly 20 centimetres in diameter, was found. Local people believe it is a dragon's bone, and it has been preserved in the monastery.

Early Walled Villages
Of all the Chinese walled villages in the New Territories, Kat Hing Wai, with its separate outer wall, corner towers and moat, is probably the most famous. Founded in the Ming Dynasty by the Tang clan, much of it has now been rebuilt. Kat Hing Wai, Wing Lung Wai and Tai Hong Wai are all walled villages of the Tang clan located in the Kam Tin valley.

These villages were built for defence against warlike neighbours, marauding bandits and pirates. One of the last 'assaults' on Kat Hing Wai was the removal of the large iron gates of the village in 1899 as a reprisal against resistance to British troops. They were returned 20 years later from the Irish estate of the Governor, Sir Henry Blake, where they had been kept.

Later Hakka walled villages, such as Sam Tung Uk, now a museum, are in fact walled compounds rather than true walled villages, as they have no separate outer wall.

Near Fanling in the district known as Lung Yeuk Tau there are a further five walled and six unwalled villages also belonging to the Tang clan. One of these, San Wai, although rather dilapidated, is notable for its superb Kun

Lung gate tower which is the best of its type in Hong Kong.

Ping Kong, another walled village to the east of the golf course at Fanling, belongs to the Hau clan.

Sam Tung Uk Folk Museum

Sam Tung Uk, a walled Hakka village in the heart of urban Tsuen Wan, was founded in 1786 by Chan Yam-shing. Several members of the Chan family migrated from their original home in Fujian Province to Guangdong in the 18th century. The Chans built sea walls, reclaimed arable land and became farmers.

When first constructed, the village consisted only of three roofed halls, of which the main supporting roof beams were called *tung*. The name Sam Tung Uk means 'three-beam dwelling'.

As the family expanded a row of houses was added to the back, front and on both sides of the original row. The village was declared a monument in 1981 and the Chans moved into modern housing. Sam Tung Uk was converted into a museum which opened in 1987.

It features traditional Hakka furniture, clothes, tools and farming implements, and several buildings house period displays and descriptions of local festivals.

Law Uk Folk Museum

Law Uk is a charming 200-year-old Hakka village house on Hong Kong Island, now surrounded by huge blocks of flats in modern Chai Wan. It has been converted into a museum with displays of traditional Hakka furniture and farming implements. Like Sam Tung Uk, Law Uk is a poignant reminder of Hong Kong's past in the midst of 20th-century development.

Ancestral Halls

The largest and most impressive ancestral halls in the New Territories belong to the five great clans. Each village may have more than one hall built for the worship of the clan's ancestors, serving different branches of the lineage. Four of the finest halls of the Tang clan date from the 17th century.

Ancestral halls, which represent the heart of Chinese villagers' religious and family life, are among the most majestic, lavishly-decorated and richly-ornamented buildings in the New Territories.

Sam Tung Uk, Tsuen Wan (left above); the entrance to Kat Hing Wai walled village in the Kam Tin valley, New Territories (left below); the interior of a Hakka village house (above); playing cards, Law Uk Folk Museum, Chai Wan (below)

Many of their roofs are adorned with porcelain figures and friezes from the Shek Wan kilns in Guangdong Province. Inside, eaves and roof brackets are delicately carved with depictions of plants, flowers, animals and legendary figures. Some halls have stone columns and finely-painted frescoes, and many are guarded by stone lions at the entrance.

Ancestral halls may consist of as many as three chambers with open courtyards between. In the innermost hall the soul tablets of the ancestors rest on the altar. Outside the front door there is often a wall to prevent evil spirits from entering the building.

Two of the finest ancestral halls in the New Territories, dating from the 17th and 18th centuries, are Man Lun-fung, belonging to the Man clan at San Tin, and Liu Man Shek Tong, belonging to the Lius at Sheung Shui.

Study Libraries

The richer clans in the New Territories, both Punti and Hakka, established study libraries in their villages for the cleverest of their sons to study for the imperial civil service examinations. Instructed by a tutor employed by the clan, the young men studied literary composition (called the 'eight-legged essay') and the Confucian classics, to prepare for the examinations that would qualify them as scholars and officials. Those who passed the examinations brought great prestige to their families; they themselves were exempted from official labour or punishment by the lash, received courteously by officials, and given special privileges by the clan.

There were various levels of degree. The examinations for the highest degree of *jinshi* were held in Peking, while the middle degree of *juren* was sat for in provincial capitals. The lowest degree of *shengyuan* was examined at district level.

Between 1573 and 1819 Xin-an County produced 62 *juren*; of these, ten continued their studies and eventually obtained the *jinshi* degree. However, a system of purchasing degrees began during the Ming Dynasty, resulting in a great many *shengyuan* first-degree holders, not all of whom were genuine scholars.

Clan schools ceased to function at the beginning of the 20th century, following the abolition of the imperial examinations in 1905. Children in the New Territories were

Gong rack at the Hau Wong temple, Yuen Long

40

educated instead in schools provided by religious bodies and the British administration.

The oldest study library is Chou Wong Yi Kwong Shue Yuen at Kam Tin, built originally as an ancestral hall in honour of the two Guangdong officials responsible for encouraging the lifting of the coastal evacuation order in the 17th century.

Tsui Shing Lau Pagoda

The Tsui Shing Lau pagoda at Ping Shan, dating from the 14th century, is Hong Kong's only ancient pagoda. Pagodas are traditionally Buddhist structures, but they were also built to improve the geomantic influences of a locality. According to members of the Tang clan, Tsui Shing Lau ('Building of Many Stars') is a geomantic *feng shui* structure, designed to ward off evil influences from the north and to encourage scholarship.

Hexagonal in shape, the pagoda is ten metres wide and 20 metres high. Originally it had seven storeys, four of which have now disappeared, probably as the result of damage by typhoons. The names of the storeys are 'The Milky Way is frozen', 'Gathering star chamber' and 'The light shines half way down the way'.

Tin Hau Temples

Of the many temples in the territory honouring different deities, those built for worship of Tin Hau, Goddess of Heaven, are amongst the oldest and most interesting.

According to legend Tin Hau was the sixth daughter of an official called Lin Yuan, who lived in Fujian Province. She was born in the early years of the Song Dynasty. At the age of 15, after finding a pair of bronze amulets in a well, Tin Hau acquired the ability to go into a trance, to predict the future and to ride on clouds. She gained a reputation for saving many people in danger, especially those at sea.

When she was 28 years old, Tin Hau climbed a hill with her sisters. Seeing a beautiful carriage in the sky, Tin Hau said goodbye to them and rode up to heaven in the carriage. The people of Fujian honoured her as a goddess and local sailors, in particular, have sought her protection at sea ever since.

The Tin Hau temple at Joss House Bay is believed to date from the 13th century, towards the end of the Song Dynasty,

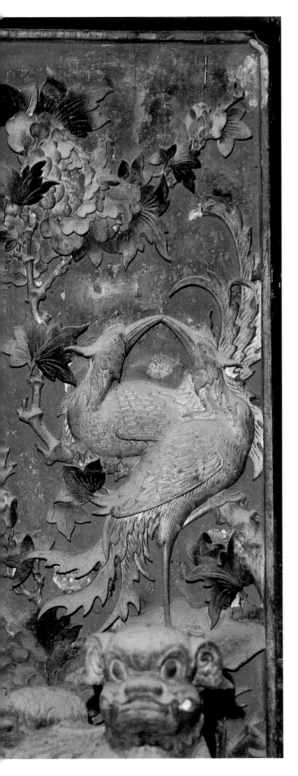

Tsang Tai Uk, Sha Tin (left); carved door from Tang Ancestral Hall, Ping Shan (middle); roof detail from Liu Man Shek Tong Ancestral Hall, Sheung Shui (top right); roof detail from Man Lun Fung Ancestral Hall, San Tin (middle right); Tang Ancestral Hall, Ping Shan (bottom right)

but it is thought to have been rebuilt several times. The original building was erected by two brothers named Yun, who were ship-owners.

The brothers were shipwrecked in a storm but they managed to survive by clinging to the sails of their ship and clutching a tablet inscribed in memory of Tin Hau. Grateful to the goddess for saving their lives, the Yuns built a large temple for her worship on Tung Lung Island. This temple no longer exists.

However a second temple to Tin Hau, on the opposite shore at Joss House Bay, was built some years later by the son of one of the Yun brothers. Sadly, the present temple, which was probably not the original, was seriously damaged in 1962 during Typhoon Wanda, though it has been completely renovated.

The earliest of Hong Kong's many Tin Hau temples were built in the 17th century at Causeway Bay, Fanling and Yuen Long. There are four further temples dedicated to Tin Hau dating from the 18th century: two on Cheung Chau, one at Fan Lau on Lantau, and one at Kam Tin in the New Territories. In all, the Antiquities and Monuments Office has graded 19 Tin Hau temples as buildings of historical interest.

The site of the oldest temple on Hong Kong Island is at Ma Hang in Stanley. However, the present Ma Hang temple is not the original, having been built on the site of its 200-year-old predecessor in 1938. While the temple itself is modern, the ancient bell and drum belonging to the pirate chief, Cheung Po-tsai, have remained intact. They stand at the back of the main hall on the right. An inscription on the bell tells us it was cast in 1767 by a smith in Canton. Apparently Cheung Po-tsai established his headquarters at Stanley and used the bell and drum, located on a small promontory, to send signals to his pirate fleet.

When Stanley was attacked by the Japanese during the Second World War, the villagers took refuge in the temple. During fierce bombardment from the sea, two shells hit the temple but neither exploded. The villagers attributed their salvation to the miraculous intercession of Tin Hau.

Later, during the Japanese occupation, a tiger attacked a Stanley resident near the temple. Troops shot the animal and the villagers hung its skin in the temple as an offering to Tin Hau. It remains there to this day.

The ancient Tsui Shing Lau Pagoda at Ping Shan, New Territories (left)

Hau Wong Temples

There are four temples in the territory dedicated to Hau Wong: one each in Kowloon City and Yuen Long, and two on Lantau at Tung Chung and Tai O.

Hau Wong (Prince Marquis) was the title accorded to Yang Liang-jie, the uncle of the Song boy emperors. Yang protected his wards to the best of his ability during their tumultuous stay in Hong Kong. He died in Kowloon and the temple was erected there in his honour in 1731.

The Hau Wong temple at Tung Chung is thought to date from 1777, the Yeung Hau (Marquis Yang) temple at Tai O from 1699 and the Yeung Hau temple in Yuen Long from 1811.

Wun Yiu Kilns

Wun Yiu, meaning 'Bowl Kiln', is the name of a village in the hills south of Tai Po. The pottery kilns at Sheung Wun Yiu are believed to have been in use as long ago as the 17th century. Production ceased at the beginning of this century.

A carved boat at the Tin Hau temple, Joss House Bay (above right); Tin Hau temple interior, Stanley (below right); Pat Heung Temple, Yuen Long, New Territories (above); Hau Wong Temple, Yuen Long (below)

The Wun Yiu kilns were associated with other kilns in Guangdong Province producing similar widely-used wares. Remains of two kilns and dumps of pottery débris are visible in a fenced-off area.

Nearby, in the grounds of the school at Sheung Wun Yiu, is the Fan Sing Kung, a temple built in 1790. Fan Sing is the patron god of potters, and workers at the kilns are believed to have worshipped there.

Qing Forts

There are four Chinese forts dating from the Qing Dynasty to be found in Hong Kong: one on Tung Lung Island and three on the west and south coasts of Lantau, at Tung Chung and Fan Lau.

The fort at Tung Lung is the oldest, built on the site of a lookout station on the northeastern tip of the island. Constructed between 1719 and 1724 by order of Yang Lin, Viceroy of Guangdong and Guangxi, it guarded the strategic Fat Tong Mun eastern passage through Hong Kong harbour which was used by junks sailing to Canton.

Despite being remote and difficult to maintain, the fort was manned until 1810 by a small detachment of soldiers. According to the San On gazetteer the detachment, whose task was to suppress piracy, comprised one officer, 25 men

and eight cannon. Communication with other forts in the area was by relayed smoke signals. The detachment was withdrawn from Tung Lung when a new, more accessible fort was built on the Kowloon Peninsula.

Measuring 22.5 x 33.5 metres, the fort consists of a central courtyard surrounded by 11 small rooms with high ramparts on all sides. Excavation of the ruins started in 1979. More than 10,000 pieces of pottery were found, but only a few military artefacts. All items of use and value were probably removed when the soldiers departed. The fabric of the structure has been stabilised and partially restored.

Tung Lung Island is sparsely populated, rugged and beautiful. There is a private ferry to the island from Shau Kei Wan, operating at weekends.

The dimensions of the fort at Tung Chung on Lantau are much larger, measuring 60 x 80 metres. The date 1832 is carved on the slab over the entrance, but it is mentioned in local records as early as 1817. The garrison comprised one 'commander-in-chief', three officers and 150 soldiers.

On the evidence of its massive ramparts for cannon, the fort must have had strategic significance. On the north wall there are six muzzle-loading cannon with Chinese inscriptions, two dating from 1805 and 1809 and two from 1843. However, it is described as a 'military administrative centre' in Chinese records and, being situated well back from the sea on low ground, its function was probably that of a command centre exercising control over other forts in the area, rather than primarily the control of shipping off the west coast of Lantau.

Tung Chung fort at present houses the local primary school and local government offices.

The solid walls of Tung Chung battery (so named to distinguish it from Tung Chung fort) were discovered in 1980 in dense undergrowth on a nearby slope overlooking the sea. This fort is thought to be one of the forts controlled by the main Tung Chung fort. However Tung Chung battery has yet to be excavated so its exact age is not known.

Fan Lau fort, mentioned in the *San On* gazetteer as 'Kai Yi Kok fort', is located on the southern tip of Lantau overlooking the sea. Long disused, little is known about the fort at Fan Lau, but it was probably one of a string of forts in the Pearl River estuary. It was described by the British in

1841 as being in ruins, but Chinese records state that it was manned until 1898 when Lantau was leased to the British as part of the New Territories.

Fan Lau fort has been repaired and restored and is worth a visit although it is a long way from the main road.

Inscriptions

The oldest known inscription in Hong Kong with a precise date is the Song Dynasty carving at Joss House Bay, located on a huge boulder behind the Tin Hau temple. It comprises 108 characters in nine vertical columns and dates from 1274.

Composed by a salt official, Yen I-chang, who was based at Guanfu on the Kowloon Peninsula, the inscription commemorates his visit to Joss House Bay. It refers to his inspection of the completed renovation of the Tin Hau temples on either side of the Fat Tong Mun passage. These temples were located at Joss House Bay and on Tung Lung

Cannons at Tung Chung Fort, north Lantau

Island and had been repaired by certain individuals from Fuzhou, Quanzhou and Wenzhou.

The Sung Wong Toi carving in Kowloon relates to the boy emperors' sojourn in Hong Kong, but it was probably carved in the Yuan Dynasty. The characters, originally inscribed on a boulder overlooking Kowloon Bay, mean 'Terrace of the Song Kings'.

During the Second World War the boulder was fractured when the hill was being levelled for an extension to the airport, but the part bearing the characters survived. After the war the Hong Kong Government installed this section of boulder in a small park and named a nearby road Sung Wong Toi Road.

The inscription *kao shan dai yat* at Castle Peak is discussed in the section on Castle Peak Monastery (page 37).

The two Li family taxation-stones found on Lantau bear rather more mundane inscriptions. On the flat top of each one are carved two characters for 'House of Li'; and on each of the four vertical sides are inscribed characters meaning 'taxable mountain land'.

One stone was found in 1955 lying in the undergrowth at Silvermine Bay and the other was found at Man Kok Tsui, near Silvermine Bay, still planted in the ground. Scholars believe the stones mark the boundaries of land awarded to a Cantonese official, Li Mao-ying, in 1265. There may be further stones of this kind, as yet undiscovered.

One of the Li taxation-stones is now displayed in a small garden near the Silvermine Bay ferry terminal and the other is housed by the Museum of History in Kowloon Park.

Boulder Trackways
Boulder trackways are described as 'Chinese roads about four foot wide and mostly paved' on very early British maps of the New Territories. The trackways follow the natural lines of communication across passes and along ridges and are probably of great antiquity.

The network of ancient paved roads provides evidence of how Hong Kong's early villages were interconnected and also of the organisation required in quarrying the stones and transporting them to remote places.

The main trackways run from Luk Keng, at the eastern end of the border with Shenzhen, to Tsat Muk Kiu; from

Mau Ping to Pak Kong, in Sai Kung; from Ngong Ping to Shek Pik, on Lantau; from Tai Lam Chung in the northwestern New Territories to Pat Heung; and from Yi O to Fan Lau on Lantau.

Stone Circles

K M A Barnett, District Commissioner for the New Territories, first noticed the stone circle in the northern part of Lamma Island in 1956. Twenty-eight large stones lie buried in the earth on a slope 100 metres above sea level. They form two overlapping circles measuring 2.5 x 3 metres.

In 1980 a second circle, or rather an oval, was found on Lantau at Fan Lau, 40 metres above sea level overlooking a small bay. The age and significance of the circles are not known.

SETTLEMENT BY THE BRITISH
19TH-CENTURY COLONIAL HONG KONG

On 25th January 1841 Captain Charles Elliot, Royal Navy, landed on Hong Kong Island and planted the Union flag at Possession Point, claiming Hong Kong as a colony for the United Kingdom. Rather than the 'barren island' envisaged by Lord Palmerston, a more accurate description of Hong Kong at that time might be that of a quiet backwater of the Manchu empire, troubled only by pirates and local disputes.

With a total population of 7,450, the island Elliot took over was very different from Hong Kong today. As we have seen, both Punti and Hakka farmers had long been cultivating fertile valleys on the island and elsewhere in the region. Chek Chue (Stanley), with 2,000 people, was the largest of Hong Kong's 16 villages, followed by Shau Kei Wan with 1,200.

However, we must look at why the British felt compelled to occupy Hong Kong Island, and the causes of their dispute with the Chinese officials controlling trade in Canton.

A fundamental difficulty for British merchants was that for more than 100 years Britain had wished to trade with China on an equal basis; but China had felt self-sufficient and did not desire products from other countries. Although foreign trade was tolerated, it was conducted according to rules established by Chinese officials in Canton.

The British found these rules restrictive and irksome. For example, direct communication between Chinese officials and Europeans was forbidden as the Chinese considered Europeans to be 'barbarians'. Business had to take place through intermediaries, called the Hong merchants, who had a monopoly on trade. Moreover, the officials frequently levied arbitrary customs duties.

Foreigners were allowed to live in Canton only between October and May. The Chinese isolated them in the 'factory' area of the city, in the Western suburbs, and forbade them to bring their wives to live with them.

In order to balance imports of tea, silk and porcelain from China, British traders from the East India Company sold opium from India to traders who in turn sold it to the Chinese at Canton and elsewhere along the coast. Although illegal, this was often done with the connivance of Chinese officials.

Problems arose when the authorities in Peking realised that payments for opium were causing an ever-increasing outflow of silver from China, and they sought to put an end to the trade. Britain had little sympathy with Chinese demands to cease their activities, since the Chinese authorities did not consistently enforce measures to prevent their own officials and merchants from participating in and profiting from the traffic.

Another difficulty was that the Chinese refused to give diplomatic recognition to representatives of the British government. Eventually Britain came to the conclusion that China would only agree to a commercial treaty if threatened by the use of force.

In frustration they considered buying, or negotiating for, an island off the China coast that would serve both as a naval base and a trading post. It could function as a replacement for Canton, and would be a place where British law and order could prevail.

The train of events that led to Hong Kong's cession to Britain began with the appointment in 1839 of Commissioner Lin in Canton. Lin's task was to suppress the traffic in opium. He acted speedily and directly by ordering the surrender of all opium in the hands of foreign merchants. The 'factory' area was besieged and Captain Elliot, the British Superintendent of Trade, eventually agreed to hand over more than 20,000 chests of opium.

However, Elliot refused to accept Lin's new terms of trade and the British merchants withdrew from Canton to Macau, and from there to Hong Kong harbour. When a Chinese was killed in a brawl by a British shore party, Lin demanded that his murderer be handed over to China. The British refused; the Chinese attacked their ships with fire-rafts; and the British Foreign Secretary, Lord Palmerston,

Captain Charles Elliot

53

Sir Henry Pottinger, c 1850, Governor of Hong Kong 1841-44 (above); The Times *newspaper, London, announces the cession of Hong Kong Island to the British Government, November 1842 (right)*

CHINA.

PEACE CONCLUDED.

EXTRAORDINARY EXPRESS FROM PARIS.

THE TIMES-OFFICE, Monday, 5 o'clock a.m.

We have this moment received by express the Paris papers of Saturday night, with a letter from our correspondent.

The *Messager* says :—" The following intelligence, received by express (the telegraph, no doubt), has been communicated to us :—

"ALEXANDRIA, Nov. 5.

" A treaty of peace has been concluded between the British Plenipotentiary and the Chinese Government, the principal articles of which are—

" 1. China will pay in three years 21,000,000 of dollars.

" The ports of Canton, Amoy, Ningpo, and two others, are open to British commerce.

"3. The island of Hongkong is ceded for ever to Her Britannic Majesty.

"4. The prisoners taken will be restored.

"5. An amnesty shall be proclaimed.

" 6. The officers of the two nations shall be treated on a footing of equality.

" 7. The islands of Chusan and of Golong-Soo shall be occupied until the tribute shall have been paid."

---

decided the time had come to take action.

What Palmerston demanded from the Chinese was compensation for the opium that had been seized; security and freedom of commerce for British subjects in China; and the cession of one or more islands that would serve as trading stations. An expeditionary force was dispatched to blockade Canton, the mouth of the Yangtze and the river leading to Peking. When the force reached the north, the Chinese agreed to negotiate.

The negotiations took place in Canton. Agreement on more favourable terms of trade had almost been arrived at when the talks broke down at the last minute. Unfortunately, Elliot had already announced the terms of the settlement but no agreement was ever signed. Undeterred, Elliot went ahead and occupied Hong Kong. Hostilities continued but Palmerston considered Elliot had disobeyed his instructions, as he had failed to secure a formal treaty with the Chinese and his occupation of Hong Kong had failed to give Britain full sovereignty over the island.

Palmerston was furious and Elliot was recalled to England. Both Elliot and his opposite number in Canton, Kishen, were in disgrace. Elliot was posted as Chargé d'Affaires to the Republic of Texas and Kishen was sent to Tibet.

The new British Superintendent of Trade, Sir Henry Pottinger, arrived in Hong Kong with specific instructions to secure either an island trading-station on the east coast of China, or permission for British merchants to conduct trade from Chinese ports, and for British consuls to reside there. However, after Pottinger had been in Hong Kong a short time, he became convinced that Britain should keep the island.

Meanwhile warfare continued: the British attacked Shanghai, blockaded the Grand Canal and in the summer of 1842 they reached Nanking. In order to save the city the Chinese agreed to Pottinger's demands. They paid $21 million dollars in compensation for the seized opium; they agreed to diplomatic equality between Britain and China; five ports were opened to British consuls and merchants; prisoners held by both sides were released; customs tariffs were agreed; and, finally, Hong Kong Island was ceded to Britain in perpetuity. The Treaty of Nanking was ratified in June 1843 and Sir Henry Pottinger became Hong Kong's first governor.

The question of opium sales to China remained unsolved. In 1843 Alexander Matheson of Jardine, Matheson and Company, at that time a major opium-trader, wrote: 'The Plenipotentiary (Sir Henry Pottinger) has published a most fiery proclamation against smuggling, but I believe it is like the Chinese edicts, meaning nothing, and only meant for the saints of England. Sir Henry never means to act upon it and no doubt privately considers it a good joke. At any rate he allows the drug to be landed and stored at Hong Kong.'

Pottinger's successor, Sir John Davis, decided it would be better to create an opium monopoly in Hong Kong. The monopoly, however, proved unsatisfactory so he abolished it for a while and set up a licensing system instead. A licence to sell raw opium in Hong Kong cost $30 a month.

The Chinese authorities remained unable to prevent or control the trade. Eventually in 1858 the Treaty of Tientsin legalised opium sales in China and the drug was also taxed by the Chinese Imperial Maritime Customs.

Despite the formation in 1874 of the Anglo-Oriental

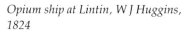

Opium ship at Lintin, W J Huggins, 1824

Society for the Suppression of the Opium Trade in England, it was not until 1891 that the first serious attempt was made by the Secretary of State for the Colonies, Lord Knutsford, to suppress opium in Hong Kong. A resolution was passed in the Houses of Parliament condemning the trade and setting up a commission of inquiry.

Finally, in 1909, the export from Hong Kong of prepared opium was forbidden to any country which prohibited its import, but use of opium remained legal in Hong Kong until the Second World War.

Let us return to the 19th century. Between 1841 and 1843, when the Treaty of Nanking was finally ratified by both the British and the Chinese governments, Hong Kong's future as a British colony remained rather uncertain. Nevertheless, Elliot began to organise its administration as a trading post and Captain Edward Belcher surveyed the island, naming many of the peaks.

Elliot issued a proclamation in February 1841 to Hong Kong's inhabitants announcing the Queen's dominion over the island and promising them: protection against all enemies; freedom to practise their own religion; government according to Chinese laws and customs by village elders, subject to the control of a British magistrate; and exemption from the payment of taxes to the British government.

Elliot invited merchants to come and trade in Hong Kong and he organised the first government land sales. Land was parcelled into marine lots (by the sea), town lots (certain areas inland) and suburban lots (all the rest). Some areas were designated as Chinese bazaars (present-day Western and Wan Chai) and some were reserved for the army and the navy (Sai Ying Pun, the former Victoria Barracks site and the present site of the new Bank of China Building as far as HMS Tamar).

Thirty years later the Reverend James Legge, famous for his translation of the Confucian Classics, recalled that in 1843:

Turning to the West where Wellington Street runs into Queen's Road you could see a few Chinese houses on either side of the latter, and Jervois Street was in course of formation, the houses on the north side of it having the waters of the bay washing about among them. Eastwards from the same point on to Pottinger Street Queen's Road was pretty well lined with Chinese houses...

Looking up Aberdeen Street you saw a few indications of building, and a house on the South of Gage Street forming the headquarters of the Madras Regiment, and looking up Pottinger Street you could see the Magistracy and Gaol of the day, where the dreaded Major Caine presided, and below them were 2 or 3 other buildings. On from Pottinger Street a few English merchants had established themselves. On the West of D'Aguilar Street (not then so named) building was going on and just opposite to it was a small house called the Bird Cage out of which was hatched the Hong Kong dispensary. All the space between Wyndham Street and Wellington Street was garden ground with an imposing flat-roofed house in it built by Mr Brain of the firm Dent and Co.

On the South of the street was the Harbour Master's establishment on Pedder's Hill — and as conspicuous as are now Messrs. Heard and Company's offices which were manufactured from it, rose the house of Mr Johnston who had been administrator of the island on its first occupancy.

On the parade ground was a small mat building, which was the Colonial Church, and above it, about where the Cathedral and Government offices now stand, were the unpretending Government offices of that early time, and the Post Office.

By 1844 the population of Hong Kong Island had grown to 20,000, with an influx of Chinese workers from the mainland seeking work. The city, formerly known as 'Queen's Town' and renamed 'Victoria' by Pottinger, grew at an astounding rate. Two years later plans were in hand for the Anglican cathedral, the cricket ground, an ice-house and government offices. Murray Barracks and Wellington Barracks were built under the supervision of General D'Aguilar together with a substantial residence for the General Officer Commanding (GOC), Flagstaff House. Jardine, Matheson and Co had settled at East Point (Causeway Bay), the Parsee community had their own cemetery at West Point; the Chinese built a new temple in Hollywood Road and a racecourse was laid out at Happy Valley.

Maintaining law and order in a community of buccaneers, entrepreneurs and scoundrels was a major problem. Apparently flogging ordered by Major Caine, the Chief Magistrate, held no terror for half-starved gaolbirds from Canton and imprisonment in the Hong Kong gaol was a welcome respite for them.

A lithograph depicting the signing of the Treaty of Tientsin, 1858, which legalised opium sales in China, artist unknown (above). The state entry of Lord Elgin into Peking, 1860, artist unknown (below)

Charles May, a London police officer was sent to Hong Kong in 1845 to form a police force. It was made up of Europeans, Indians and Chinese but for many years it was notoriously inefficient. Police stations were built at Victoria, Aberdeen and Stanley.

Hospitals too were quickly established to cope with victims of fever. In the summer of 1843, 440 European troops died and many people were seriously ill. Three newly-established hospitals overflowed with patients. A walk round the Colonial Cemetery in Happy Valley today shows how many young men succumbed to sickness and disease during the early years of the Colony.

In the ten years to 1853 the population nearly doubled, reaching over 39,000. The previous year the first reclamation of land from the harbour was begun and a new road, Bonham Strand, was named after the current governor, Sir Samuel Bonham. His successor, Sir John Bowring, continued land reclamation with the building of a *praya*, or waterfront road, along the entire seafront of the settlement, and he initiated the laying out of the Botanical Gardens.

At the beginning of 1857, relations with China hit another low, culminating in the *Arrow* War. The *Arrow* was a Chinese-owned ship, registered in Hong Kong, with a British captain. The previous October the ship had been in Canton and in the absence of the captain, was boarded by the Chinese authorities. The crew was imprisoned as pirates, and allegedly the British flag was hauled down. Bowring supported the British Consul's demand for an apology from the Chinese and when it was not forthcoming he declared war on China.

In Hong Kong political unrest was instigated by the Chinese in Canton. Apparently on the order of the mandarins, bread supplied by the E Sing bakery in Wan Chai was laced with arsenic, which resulted in serious illness for Lady Bowring and many others. There was a massive crackdown and several hundred Chinese were rounded up and deported to Hainan. George Duddell, who had previously held the opium monopoly, took over the supply of bread until his bakery was burnt down soon afterwards.

A view of Wyndham Street from the Post Office (above); Aberdeen Street looking north (below), painted by M Bruce, 1846

One of the outcomes of the *Arrow* war was the opening of five more treaty ports in China to foreign trade, ending Hong Kong's rôle as the headquarters of British trade and

influence in the Far East. Britain and China signed the Treaty of Tientsin in 1858 but war was resumed in 1859, to be settled the following year with the signing of the Convention of Peking.

Under the terms of this peace treaty the Kowloon Peninsula and Stonecutters Island were ceded outright as dependencies of the Colony of Hong Kong 'with a view to maintaining law and order in and about the Harbour of Hong Kong'.

The additional land on the Kowloon Peninsula was put to good use. By 1859 the population had reached more than 86,000. The huge influx of Chinese was caused partly by the Taiping Rebellion on the mainland and partly by Hong Kong's growing prosperity. To a limited extent immigration was offset by Chinese emigration to North America and Australia with the gold rushes of 1849 and 1851. Emigration also resulted from the illegal trade in coolie labour for the West Indies.

When the newly-constructed dry dock at Whampoa near Canton was destroyed in 1857, the Governor, Sir John Bowring, proposed that a dock should be built in Hong Kong for ship repairs, the chief customer being the Royal Navy. The Lamont dock at Aberdeen was completed in 1860 and the Hope dock constructed next to it was opened in 1867. A typhoon demolished both docks in 1874, but with the acquisition of the Kowloon Peninsula, docks were also built at Hung Hom and Tai Kok Tsui.

From the 1860s to the end of the century Hong Kong's urban areas expanded in line with the population, which increased from 160,000 in 1881 to 260,000 in 1900. The Chinese and foreign communities lived in separate locations distinguished not on purely racial grounds but by the types of houses that could be built there. More houses of a lower standard were allowed to be built closer together in the Chinese areas. Technically, Chinese could live in European areas if they conformed with the more stringent housing regulations. This rarely happened on the Peak, although many wealthy Chinese lived in the European areas of Mid-levels. It was not until after the Second World War that this policy was abandoned.

In the 19th century the Chinese bazaars were tightly packed and, in the eyes of Hong Kong's administrators, very insanitary. Outbreaks of plague and cholera were

A 1930s Chinese bazaar in Bonham Road, Hong Kong Island

frequent. In 1867 the Governor, Sir Richard Macdonnell, established his summer residence on the Peak in what had been an army sanitorium. He and his medical officers thought that in the torrid summer months the markedly cooler climate was so much healthier that they encouraged European settlement on the hilltop. The leading merchants soon made their homes on the Peak, and the Peak Tramway was opened in 1888. The European Reservation Ordinance, limiting residence on the Peak to Europeans, was passed the same year and it remained in force until the Second World War.

Under the governorship of Sir Arthur Kennedy more land was reclaimed from the harbour on the Island's northern shore in the area now known as Kennedy Town. Kennedy is also remembered for the establishment of the Gardens and Afforestation Department and his programme of tree-planting on the Island. A statue of Kennedy was erected in the Botanical Gardens, the only governor on which this honour has been bestowed, but it was demolished by the Japanese during the occupation.

Three further reclamation schemes were undertaken in the 19th century. The swamps of Causeway Bay and Yau Ma Tei were drained in 1883 and the huge Central Reclamation Scheme was begun in 1890, to be finished in 1904. The western section of the old waterfront road in Central was renamed Des Voeux Road, after the Governor, and east of it, Chater Road was named after Sir Paul Chater, the Legislative Councillor who initiated the scheme. The new waterfront road was named Connaught Road after the Duke of Connaught.

The main thoroughfares of Central were first lit by gas lamps in 1865, and by 1890 Hong Kong had electric street lighting. The original gas lamps on D'Aguilar Street, though now electrified, are still in place. In 1875, at the instigation of the Chamber of Commerce, lighthouses were erected at Cape D'Aguilar, Green Island and Cape Collinson.

The Russian playwright, Anton Chekhov, visited Hong Kong in 1890 and wrote to his friend Alexei Suvorin:

The first foreign port on my journey was Hong Kong. It has a glorious bay, the movement of ships on the ocean is beyond anything I have seen in pictures, excellent roads, trolleys, a railway to the mountains, museums, botanical gardens; wherever

64

you turn you will note evidences of the most tender solicitude on the part of the English for men in their service; there is even a sailors' club. I drove around in a rickshaw, i.e., was borne by humans, bought all sorts of rubbish from the Chinese and got indignant listening to my Russian travelling companions abusing the English for exploiting the natives. Thought I to myself, yes, the English exploit the Chinese, the Sepoys and the Hindus, but they do give them roads, plumbing and Christianity; you exploit them too, but what do you give them?

During the 19th century the garrison played a major rôle in Hong Kong, both in its visible physical presence and in the running of the Colony. The General Officer Commanding (GOC) served as a member of the Executive Council and also held the post of Lieutenant Governor.

From the very beginning the armed forces occupied key areas in the city of Victoria (now Central); in the valley and on the hill to the east of the site now occupied by Garden Road and Cotton Tree Drive (Murray Barracks and Victoria Barracks); above Queens's Road Central (Murray Battery is commemorated by Battery Path); and the site of HMS Tamar, Admiralty and as far east as the Police Headquarters (North Barracks, the Dockyard and Wellington Barracks).

Batteries and forts were also established on Kellett Island in the harbour; Belcher's Gardens in Western (Belcher's Battery); Sai Ying Pun (occupied by Indian troops and the Naval Stores and called West Point); Sai Wan on the eastern end of the Island; Aberdeen (Shek Pai Wan) and the present site of St Stephen's College at Stanley, to the south.

The barracks at Sai Wan and Stanley were only occupied for a few years and then abandoned, since troops stationed there were decimated by malaria and typhoid. In 1849 the Governor, Sir Samuel Bonham, recommended a reduction in the Colony's military strength to six British companies and three companies of Ceylon Rifles. He considered the defence of Hong Kong rested ultimately on the Navy and he proposed that a frigate and a steamer should be permanently stationed in the Colony.

Pirates preying on shipping in Hong Kong waters were a constant problem. Not all of them were Chinese. A famous English renegade, William Fenton, was eventually brought to trial in 1851, sentenced to three years' hard labour and then deported. An American pirate, Eli Boggs,

Chinese policeman, Hollywood Road, Central police station, 1906

was tried for murder and piracy in 1857 and deported.

With the acquisition of Kowloon and Stonecutters Island in 1861 the Army built Whitfield Barracks (now Kowloon Park) and the Navy gained a site for coal storage. In 1887 the Navy took over the North Barracks site in Central (the western end of HMS Tamar) and the Army bought the Mount Austin Hotel on the Peak for use as accommodation. The Army moved into barracks at Gun Club Hill in Kowloon in 1896.

As tension increased in the 1880s between the Western powers in the Far East, the defence of Hong Kong harbour was of paramount concern. By the end of the 19th century the art of gunnery had improved enormously. Hong Kong now had to be defended with bigger guns, possessing greater range and accuracy, against attackers from further afield. The greatest threat was thought to be bombardment from the large armoured battleships of nations such as France or Russia.

Mount Davis, early 1900s

Heavy defence works were begun at Lyemun at the eastern end of the Island, together with the installation of six-inch guns and the very latest and most secret weapon, the Brennan torpedo. An ordinance was passed in 1890 making Stonecutters Island, a fortress in the harbour, a military reserved area.

The Hong Kong Volunteer Corps, which had been recruited and disbanded several times in the previous 40 years, was put on a firmer footing in 1882. Two artillery companies were formed, commanded by a regular officer from the garrison, and later a machine-gun corps was added.

Britain's desire to extend Hong Kong's boundaries to include the area known as the New Territories was aimed at ensuring the adequate defence of the Colony against other European powers. Since China, in her weakened state posed no threat, the northern border with China was left unfortified.

The 99-year lease of the New Territories was obtained as a result of successful negotiations conducted by the British Minister in Peking, Sir Claude MacDonald. The lease took effect on 1 July 1898.

With the acquisition of the New Territories, massive 9.2-inch guns were positioned at Devil's Peak covering the southeastern approaches, and at Mount Davis, guarding Hong Kong's southwestern flank. They could now engage targets more than 15 kilometres distant, whereas those at Lyemun were only able to cope with aggressors at closer range. Hong Kong had become a mighty fortress.

MONUMENTS FROM 19TH-CENTURY COLONIAL HONG KONG

HONG KONG ISLAND

Flagstaff House

Flagstaff House was known until 1932 as Headquarters House and is one of the two oldest British buildings in Hong Kong. It was built by the Royal Engineers and completed in 1846. Flagstaff House was first occupied in 1846 by Major General D'Aguilar, Officer Commanding Her Britannic Majesty's Land Forces in China. During the Japanese occupation it was the residence of a Japanese admiral.

After the Second World War, Flagstaff House continued to be used as the residence of the Commander British Forces until 1978 when it was given to the Hong Kong Government, together with the surrounding Victoria *Flagstaff House Museum of Tea Ware* Barracks site.

In 1984 the gracious and elegant mid-Victorian colonial building was renamed the Flagstaff House Museum of Tea Ware and opened to the public. Today it provides a home for Dr K S Lo's extensive collection of Chinese tea ware.

Murray House

Murray House was designed by Major Aldrich and Lieutenant Collinson of the Royal Engineers and constructed at the same time as Flagstaff House. It was a well-proportioned, three-storey building of timber and stone. Its deep verandahs were intercepted by Doric and Ionic columns and the roof was covered with Chinese tiles. Murray House served as an Officers' Mess from 1846 to 1963, when it was handed over to the Hong Kong Government.

During the Second World War the building was used by the Japanese as an interrogation centre. From 1963 onwards Murray House housed the Hong Kong Government's Rating and Valuation Department. In the 1970s its occupants thought the building was affected by a poltergeist, and a ceremony of exorcism was performed, reportedly with complete success.

The Hong Kong Government dismantled Murray House in 1982 to make way for the new Bank of China building. There was widespread criticism of the Government's 'vandalism' and in reponse, the Government proposed to re-erect the building close to the original site. Since 1982 the stones of Murray House have been stored in sheds on the edge of Tai Tam Reservoir.

In 1988 the Government decided the building should be re-erected by the Housing Authority in Ma Hang village at Stanley, and used as an amenity centre for a new low-cost housing estate.

Government House

After many delays, construction of Government House was completed in 1855 according to plans prepared by Hong Kong's Surveyor-General, Charles St G Cleverly. It was first occupied by Sir John Bowring, the Colony's fourth governor. Previous governors had made their homes in a variety of temporary residences, including a house on the waterfront at Spring Gardens, now commemorated by Spring Garden Lane in Wan Chai.

The ballroom was added in 1891, electric lighting was installed at the end of the century and in 1908 the building was cooled by electric fans. Further renovations in 1926 extended the ballroom and added a conservatory, but by the beginning of the Second World War the residence was in need of extensive repairs.

Lieutenant-General Rensuke Isogai, the Japanese governor of Hong Kong during the occupation, decided to remodel the building, incorporating traditional Japanese architecture. Designed by Seichi Fujimura, the dominant feature of the new Government House was the central tower linking the ballroom annexe and the main building. Japanese ceramic tiles adorned the roofs.

After the war the Japanese bedrooms and bathrooms were rebuilt to British design, the *tatami* mats were removed, and the first post-war governor, Sir Mark Young, reoccupied Government House.

St John's Cathedral

The foundation stone of the Cathedral Church of St John the Evangelist in Garden Road was laid by the Governor, Sir John Davis, in 1847 and the first service was held in the new building exactly two years later.

Constructed of Canton bricks in the shape of a cross, the design of the Cathedral incorporates features from 13th-century Early English, Decorated Gothic and Norman architecture. There is a bell-tower at the western end, completed a few years after the main body of the Cathedral. The chancel was extended in 1873, providing an extra 64 seats for the growing congregation. The foundation stone for the extension was laid by Prince Alfred, Queen Victoria's second son.

During the Second World War the Cathedral was used as a social club by the Japanese. By 1945 the building had lost its stained-glass windows, the altar, and the choir stalls; and the organ, the Lady Chapel, the font and the bell tower were in ruins.

During the next ten years the congregation rallied round and a programme of restoration was begun. The Lady Chapel was reconstructed in 1958 and the mosaic on the floor by the main entrance was laid in 1968.

St John's Cathedral, Central (below); Bank of China towering over Government House (right)

70

Bishop's House

The first Colonial Chaplain of Hong Kong, the Reverend Vincent Stanton, intended that Bishop's House should be used as a school for Chinese students to train as priests. The building was completed in 1848 and it housed St Paul's College until after the Second World War, when the College moved to premises in Bonham Road.

When the Diocese of Victoria was created in 1849 Bishop's House also served as the residence of the first bishop, the Right Reverend George Smith, and was extensively remodelled. It functioned as both school and bishop's residence for the next 100 years.

The interior of the building has been greatly altered and modernised but the exterior is original.

Chinese Temples

The Man Mo temple in Hollywood Road, thought to be built around 1842, is dedicated to the gods of literature (Man) and war (Mo). It is the temple most frequently visited by tourists. The God of War, with his executioner's sword, is worshipped by policemen, pawnbrokers and antique dealers. The God of Literature, the patron of civil servants, has a writing brush. The huge brass deer on the altar symbolise long life and wealth.

Inside the temple there are three antique carved-teak sedan chairs in glass cases. One is dated 1862 and is embossed in gold; the second, made in 1885 is inlaid with mother-of-pearl; and the third is shaped like a normal chair. The temple bell was cast in Canton in 1847.

To the east of Central, the Pak Tai and Hung Shing temples in Wan Chai were both built in the 1860s. Pak Tai is the Emperor of the North. According to legend, the Jade Emperor appointed him as commander of the 12 heavenly legions to fight the Demon King. The Demon King conjured up a grey tortoise and a giant serpent to assist him, but Pak Tai managed to overcome them. He is now depicted with a tortoise and a snake beneath his feet symbolising his victory over evil. The temple has a huge copper image of Pak Tai which, according to an inscription, was made in 1604.

The tiny Hung Shing temple is built with boulders from

Part of the Man Mo Temple complex in Yau Ma Tei; the inscription reads 'God of the Community'

the hillside extending right into the side and the back of the hall. The inscription on the stone altar indicates there may have been a temple here as early as 1847, but further inscriptions on the masonry reveal that this building was probably constructed in the 1860s.

Hung Hei is thought to have been a virtuous official in the Tang Dynasty who encouraged the study of astronomy, geography and mathematics. There is another temple dedicated to Hung Shing on Ap Lei Chau which was built in 1888 and, further afield, there are temples for his worship on Cheung Chau (1813) and at Sheung Shui (1860). At Ping Shan and Kam Tin near Yuen Long there are Hung Shing temples dating from the 18th century.

French Mission Building
The French Mission Building, overlooking the Hilton Hotel, stands on the site of what was arguably the first Government House — the house belonging to A R Johnston, the Deputy Superintendent of Trade, who administered the Colony in 1841 in Elliot's absence. Johnston's first house was blown down in a typhoon.

His second house was built the following year, and it was later occupied by A Heard and Co and by T G Linstead. Some time before 1860 it was enlarged from a two-storey to a three-storey building with a basement, and two corner towers were added.

Records show that in 1879 the building was owned by Emmanuel Belilios, Director of the Hongkong and Shanghai Bank, and it is believed he was responsible for reconstructing the façade. Belilios renamed the building 'Beaconsfield', after the newly-ennobled Prime Minister, Benjamin Disraeli.

The French Mission Building

Beaconsfield was taken over by the French Mission in 1915 and extensively altered. A chapel was built in the northwest corner with a cupola projecting above the roof. After the Second World War in August 1945 the French Mission building was used briefly as the headquarters of the provisional Hong Kong Government.

The missionaries sold their Hong Kong headquarters to the Government in 1953 and it then housed the Education Department and, later, Victoria District Court. Between 1980 and 1983 it was occupied by the Supreme Court. The building is currently occupied by Government Information Services.

Bethanie

Situated just off Pokfulam Road, overlooking the Lamma Channel and close to the former Nazareth House (see University Hall, below), La Maison de Béthanie was built by the French Mission in 1875 to serve as a hospital for sick missionaries from China. In 1884 it had 43 patients in residence.

A striking neo-Gothic chapel, designed by Father Osouf who later became Archbishop of Tokyo, can be seen from Pokfulam Road. Inside the former sanitorium, the main staircase has extremely low, shallow steps up to the first floor, apparently in order that the priests could glide upstairs without tripping over their long habits.

Bethanie currently serves as the offices of Hong Kong University Press and, stripped of its stained-glass windows, the chapel contains library stocks.

Roman Catholic Cathedral

The first Roman Catholic Cathedral was built in 1842 in Wellington Street. The present Cathedral of the Immaculate Conception in Caine Road dates from 1889 and is of continental Gothic design. The fine stained-glass west windows were imported from Toulouse in France at the beginning of the century. Two altars on either side of the north entrance belong to the first cathedral, which was twice damaged by fire. Many of the pillars supporting the roof were given by Portuguese members of the congregation who had come to Hong Kong from Macau.

Douglas Castle

University Hall

Originally named Douglas Castle, University Hall was built in 1861 on a hill at Pokfulam by a Hong Kong shipping magnate, John Douglas Lapraik, for use as a rural residence. With Tudor, Gothic and Colonial features — turrets, battlements and church windows — the building is imposing, ostentatious and anachronistic.

Apart from Douglas Castle, Lapraik is remembered for the clock he donated for the clock tower that used to stand at the junction of Pedder Street and Queen's Road. It was demolished in 1913.

In 1894 the Lapraik family sold Douglas Castle to the Société des Missions Étrangères de Paris, which renamed it Nazareth House. A Gothic chapel and a crypt were added by the French monks and they installed a printing press, publishing religious works in 28 languages.

The monks continued to live there during the Japanese occupation, finally selling the building in 1954 to the University of Hong Kong. It is now used as a students' hall of residence.

Western Market

The south block, constructed in 1858, was pulled down in 1980. The existing north block with four corner towers in 'bandaged' brickwork is located between Des Voeux Road and Connaught Road. It dates from 1906 and is similar in design to the older south block but a little smaller. It is a splendid example of mid-Victorian architecture.

The market used to house 12 poultry shops, a poultry-killing room, an engine room and administrative offices downstairs, and on the first floor 81 outlets for selling fish. Water for cleansing the market and for the storage of live fish was pumped by an oil engine up to two huge tanks on the roof.

Although no longer in use, plans are in hand for the renovation of Western Market for use as a period shopping centre, along the same lines as Covent Garden in England.

A painting of the Main Building, University of Hong Kong, by Brian Tilbrook, 1990

Central Police Station, Victoria Prison and Central Magistracy

Central Police Station, Victoria Prison and Central Magistracy are bounded by Arbuthnot Road, Hollywood Road and Old Bailey Street. Here Major Caine presided over Hong Kong's first gaol. By the 1860s it had become so crowded that prisoners were moved to a hulk moored in the harbour, and to Stonecutters Island.

The oldest buildings on the site date from the construction of the new gaol in 1864. These comprise a watch-tower (Bauhinia House), D Hall of the prison and the headquarters building of the police station.

A third floor was added to the headquarters building in 1905 and the four-storey extension facing onto Hollywood Road was built in 1919. The armoury to the northwest of the parade ground was constructed in 1925. Central Police Station is still occupied by the police, but after the Second World War it ceased to be the Police Headquarters.

Victoria Prison was closed in 1937 when a new prison

was completed at Stanley. However Stanley Prison quickly became overcrowded and two years later Victoria Prison was back in commission. It was badly bombed during the Second World War and it has been extensively modernised since, but it still serves its original purpose.

Completed in 1914, the majestic Central Magistracy facing onto Arbuthnot Road stands on the site of the Old Magistracy erected in 1847. The walls are of red Canton brick faced externally with Amoy bricks and the pillars of the façade are Greek-revival in style. The Arbuthnot Road entrance has a dressed granite arch and pediment but is no longer in use. There is a new entrance from the courtyard behind. The building currently houses the Hong Kong International Arbitration Centre and various police organisations.

Stanley, Peak and Aberdeen Police Stations and the Police Museum

The old Stanley Police Station was built in 1859 and it is the oldest surviving police station in Hong Kong. Its construction cost £402 16s (shillings) 2d (old pence). The building also served as the Harbour Master's Station and from time to time was used by the Army.

During the Second World War the Japanese police continued to use the building and they added on a mortuary. Stanley Police Station became a sub-office of Southern District office in 1974 and the police then moved to a new station on the other side of the road.

Before the Second World War the police station on the Peak, built in 1886, was known as Mount Gough Police Station. The old Aberdeen Police Station was built in 1891, replacing an earlier station, and was itself replaced in 1969 by a more modern building. The old Aberdeen Police Station is now used as the Marine Police Training School.

The Police Museum, opened in 1988, now stands on the site of the former Wan Chai Gap Police Station in Coombe Road.

Old Mental Hospital

The colossal, imposing façade of the former Nurses' Home, in High Street in Western, is being preserved and it will be incorporated into the new hospital to be built on the site.

The Nurses' Home was constructed in 1892 providing

Western Market

ten bedrooms, five sitting rooms and a Matron's Office for the European nursing staff, as well as extensive servants' quarters. It was used for staff accommodation until 1941 and then for the next 30 years it served as a day centre and hospital for psychiatric out-patients.

Constructed of brick with a Chinese tiled roof, the romantic two-storey building is dominated by massive arched granite verandahs with ornamental railings. It has been used frequently as a film setting.

Lei Yue Mun Park

Lei Yue Mun Park, now a holiday camp, is the site of the former Lyemun Barracks. The headland is scheduled to become a museum and the defences will soon be restored for public display.

The first barracks built in 1845 at Lyemun, commanding the Lei Yue Mun Strait, were located on the south side of the area at Sai Wan. Many of the troops stationed there were stricken by malaria and dysentery and after a few years the barracks were abandoned.

In the 1880s, with the threat of attack from other European powers, Lyemun was heavily fortified to protect Hong Kong's eastern approaches. The west, central and reverse batteries were built on the headland which was crowned by the mighty Victorian Redoubt. Originally armed with six-inch guns, the Redoubt is a honeycomb of loopholes, tunnels and lighting passages sunk into the hill and surrounded by a moat. The moat used to be straddled by a drawbridge. The west and central batteries were completed in 1887 and the reverse battery in 1890. In 1895 another battery was built at Pak Sha Wan on a low headland to the east of the Redoubt and plans were produced for the fortification of Sai Wan Hill.

Since Hong Kong was by-passed by the conflict of the First World War, the fortifications at Lyemun were never put to the test. However, in the 1930s, with the increasing possibility of attack, Lyemun fort and barracks were strengthened by the addition of new accommmodation blocks, roads and ammunition and explosives bunkers.

In 1941, when the Japanese invaded from the north, Lyemun was the scene of fierce fighting. On the night of 18 December Japanese troops landed on the Island at North Point, Taikoo and Sai Wan, and by Christmas Day the

Allies had surrendered.

After the occupation it was discovered that the Japanese had left behind a network of tunnels in the summit of Sai Wan Hill, in anticipation of attack by the Allies attempting to retake Hong Kong.

Clearing up ammunition and explosives in the area was a dangerous task. On 21 March 1946 Driver Joseph Hughes lost his life driving a lorry containing explosives which accidentally caught fire. He was awarded the George Cross posthumously for his heroic action.

By the 1950s land-based coastal defences had become obsolete. From then on, Lyemun was used as an accommodation and training base until it was handed back to the Hong Kong Government in 1987.

The Brennan Torpedo Installation

Perhaps the most exciting building at Lyemun is the Brennan torpedo installation, situated in a man-made cavern on the edge of the Lei Yue Mun Strait. In the past 100 years little has been divulged about this secret weapon of the the 1890s and it is thought only one example of the wire-guided torpedo still exists, in the museum of the Royal Engineers at Chatham in England.

The land-based torpedo was named after its inventor, Louis Brennan. It was fired across the Strait from the cavern on the edge of the water, steered by an operator on the land by means of two wires coiled on drums inside the torpedo.

Brennan demonstrated the way the torpedo worked by unwinding a reel of cotton, pulling the thread towards himself. The faster he pulled the thread the faster the cotton reel rolled in the opposite direction.

After the torpedo was launched down a ramp, the wires were reeled in onto drums rotated by high-pressure steam winches at the back of the cavern. The action of pulling the wires off the reels in the torpedo spun the torpedo's propellers.

Steering was achieved by the differential speeds at which the wires were reeled in – each drum being slowed individually with a footbrake as necessary. Containing ten kilometres of steel wire, the Brennan torpedo could travel at 50 kilometres an hour at a depth of three metres with a range of two kilometres.

In order that its course could be tracked, the torpedo carried a flag visible above the water. A lookout on the hill above instructed the operator in the cavern below which way to steer.

The Brennan torpedo was operated by the Submarine Mining Section of the Royal Engineers until it was transferred to the care of the Royal Navy in 1906. As far as we know, despite many trials, it was never fired in battle in Hong Kong.

Botanical Gardens

The Botanical Gardens were established by the Governor, Sir John Bowring, in order to spread knowledge of Chinese trees, woods and fibres. They were opened to the public in 1864 and extended in the 1870s with the addition of land bought from the infamous George Duddell.

During his term as Governor, Sir John Pope-Hennessy created the Gardens and Afforestation Sub-department which directed its energies to large-scale tree plantation on the Island. A visitor to Hong Kong in 1878 described the

A watercolour depicting the Ching Ming festival, by Tingqua (also known as Kwan Luen Cheung), 1851 - 1861

gardens as 'beautifully laid out, and where all rich and rare forms of foliage, from tropical or temperate climes, combine to produce a garden of delight'.

In 1979 the name of the gardens was changed to Hong Kong Zoological and Botanical Gardens.

Cemeteries

Traditional Chinese graves, built in the shape of an omega, are usually located on hillsides overlooking the sea, where the deceased can benefit from the best possible geomantic influences. They are easily visible on hill slopes around Hong Kong.

From the middle of the last century settlers of different faiths located their principal cemeteries in Happy Valley. The oldest is the Colonial Cemetery dating from 1845, followed by the Catholic Cemetery built in 1847, the Parsee Cemetery constructed in 1852 and the Jewish Cemetery dating from 1855.

The Colonial Cemetery has headstones in memory of the many soldiers, sailors, civil servants and missionaries who died while serving in Hong Kong, including that of Lord Napier, Britain's first Chief Superintendent of Trade with China, who died in 1834.

There are military cemeteries at Stanley and Sai Wan.

Kwong Fuk Tse Ancestral Hall

The present Kwong Fuk Tse ('Wide Blessings Public Ancestral Hall'), located in Western District, was built in 1895 to replace an earlier hall dating from 1851. It was established by local people to hold the ancestral tablets of Chinese expatriates from the mainland who had died while far away from home.

It was also used to house the sick and dying, and to store corpses in coffins before their return to the mainland for burial. Today it is a public ancestral hall with no special clan affiliations. For a fee, a dead relative's name and birthdate can be inscribed on a small wooden tablet and housed in the building for worship.

Original Hong Kong Village House

Situated in a squatter village close to the Aberdeen Tunnel and Shouson Hill, 10 –11 Wong Chuk Hang San Wai is a traditional Chinese house built in about 1890 as part of the village, Heung Kong Wai, from which Hong Kong's name is derived. This is one of only two traditional Chinese village houses remaining on Hong Kong Island, the other being Law Uk at Chai Wan.

Richly-decorated and well-maintained, this house belongs to Mrs Chow Chan Yuet-kiu. She is related to the late Sir Shouson Chow, one of Hong Kong's community leaders, after whom Shouson Hill is named.

The ancestral hall in the centre of the house is particularly fine, with a carved altar and ancestral tablets. Opposite the house there is a high *feng shui* wall built to deter evil spirits.

Octagonal Dairy Farm Cowsheds

Traditionally, Chinese people did not drink cows' milk. The Dairy Farm Company was founded in 1886 by Dr Patrick Manson to provide clean milk, free from disease and germs, to the Western community in Hong Kong. The unusual octagonal cowsheds at Pok Fu Lam were designed for easy disposal of manure and frequent washing down.

Inside the sheds the cows faced the outer walls. There was a hole in the floor in front of each one. Instructions for the cowhands were written in Chinese and hung at each stall. The Dairy Farm started with a herd of 80 cows.

Inscriptions

In 1897 two foundation stones were laid to mark Queen Victoria's Diamond Jubilee and the start of two projects bearing her name. One stood at the beginning of the new Victoria Road but was moved in 1977 to the junction of Victoria Road and Mount Davis Road. The other, the Victoria Hospital stone, stands on its original site in Barker Road on the Peak, although the hospital was pulled down many years ago.

Peak Tram

The Peak Tram, constructed in 1888 by A Findlay Smith, is a funicular railway: that is ascending and descending cars on the railway counterbalance each other. The railway is 1,370 metres in length and it rises from the lower terminal in St John's Building in Garden Road to the upper terminal at Victoria Gap, 400 metres above sea level, with five halts in between.

The first tram cars were made of wood and the haulage plant was steam-powered. The fare was 60 cents. The upper and lower terminals have been rebuilt several times and the tram cars have been completely modernised.

Before the Second World War the front section of the tram was reserved for the Governor, whose summer retreat, Mountain Lodge, was at the top of the Peak.

Duddell Street Steps and Gaslamps
The broad flight of granite steps at the upper end of Duddell Street was built some time between 1875 and 1889.

Four gas street lamps surmount each end of the balustrades. Their age is not known but similar models appear in the 1922 catalogue of Suggs and Co. The streets of Hong Kong were first lit by gas in January 1865, but electricity gradually replaced gas illumination after the Second World War.

Originally installed by the Hong Kong and China Gas Company, the lamps have been electrified and retained for historical interest.

Early days of the Peak Tram

Beas River Country Club Gateway

The gateway at Beas River Country Club originally belonged to Jardine, Matheson and Company's Number One House. This palatial building at East Point, now Causeway Bay, was constructed on land bought in Hong Kong's first land auction in 1841.

In 1923 the house was sold to Lee Hysan, a Chinese entrepreneur. The gateway was donated by Jardines to the Royal Hong Kong Jockey Club and it was re-erected as the entrance to the Beas River Country Club.

Plaques

The Antiquities and Monuments Office has erected plaques at various historic locations in the territory commemorating famous people, places and events.

At Wong Fung Ling College, in Gough Street on Hong Kong Island, there are two plaques, one marking the place where Sun Yat-sen, founder of the Chinese Republic, studied 100 years ago, and the other commemorating Dr James Legge, who taught there.

Dr José Rizal of the Philippines is commemorated by a plaque in D'Aguilar Street, and three plaques in Pedder Street mark the 19th-century waterfront in Central, showing the extent of the various reclamation schemes.

The sites of the Old City Hall and the Old Hong Kong Cricket Club are remembered by plaques in Bank Street and Jackson Road, and the Hong Kong Mint is commemorated by a plaque in Cleveland Street, Causeway Bay.

Magazine Island, Kellett Bay

Originally named One Tree Island, Magazine Island lies just to the west of Aberdeen Harbour. From 1887 to 1908 it was leased for an annual rent of $100, by the Nobel Explosives Company, who built a magazine and a road and planted trees.

Magazine Island was abandoned in 1908 when the Government completed the construction of the explosives depot on Green Island.

KOWLOON AND STONECUTTERS ISLAND

Royal Observatory

Surrounded on all sides by modern office blocks, the Royal Observatory was constructed in 1883 on top of Mount Elgin, a small, wooded hill east of Nathan Road. Dr Doberck was the first Government Astronomer.

The Observatory is an elegant, two-storey, colonial building with arched windows, columns and long verandahs, overlooking a spacious lawn surrounded by trees.

Royal Observatory staff have provided typhoon warnings, weather forecasts and meteorological data for Hong Kong for more than a century.

Marine Police Headquarters

After being housed for many years in a former opium vessel moored in the harbour, the Water Police moved into their new offices, the Marine Police Headquarters, constructed on the site of an old Chinese fort in Kowloon in 1884. They have shared the buildings, near the Star Ferry, with the Land Police of Tsim Sha Tsui District for more than 100 years.

Originally only two storeys high, the third floor of the building was added in the 1920s. There is an underground tunnel leading from the hall to the kitchen and servants' quarters. Before the Second World War the District Superintendent of Kowloon lived in the east wing. The time-ball signal tower standing in the grounds was moved to Blackhead's Hill in 1907.

During the battle for Hong Kong, the Japanese mounted guns on the front lawn to shell the Island. The building was used by the Japanese navy during the occupation and a theatre was built in the grounds. It is now used as a barrack block.

The Japanese also constructed a magazine on the lawn and air-raid tunnels in the hillside; and they left behind a steel and leather office chair, said to have been used exclusively by the Japanese admiral.

Signal Tower

The Signal Tower at Blackhead's Hill was rebuilt in 1907 to house the time-ball which had been located in the grounds

Painted doors at the Sin Shut study library (above); Hakka Wai, Sheung Shui New Territories (below)

of the Marine Police Headquarters. Ships in the harbour used to adjust their chronometers daily at 1 pm by the time signal, the dropping of a hollow copper ball suspended from the top of the tower.

The tower was three storeys high, with a spiral staircase, the mast standing more than 50 metres above sea-level. A fourth storey and a dome were added in 1927. The first floor contains the air cylinder which checks the fall of the ball and the second floor contains the hoisting machinery and the electric lock.

The last time signal from the tower was given in 1933 when it was replaced by radio signals. The building houses a small maritime museum.

Chinese Temples, Yau Ma Tei
The complex of four temples in Yau Ma Tei was built between 1870 and 1876 and at that time was only a few yards from the sea. Although it is known as the Tin Hau Temple there are in fact four temples grouped together, dedicated to a great many other gods.

The main temple is for worship of Tin Hau (Queen of Heaven) but inside this temple, in addition to various other deities, there are three shelves laden with images of the Tai Sui (the 60 gods of the year). One god represents each year of the Chinese 60-year cycle. Worshippers pray to the god whose number corresponds to their age. When the complex was refurbished in 1972 a fire broke out in the Tin Hau temple and the rafters and roof were destroyed. They have been replaced with plain modern materials.

The temple to the right belongs to Shing Wong (the city god). Further to the right is the Fook Tak temple, honouring To Tei (the Earth God) and Kwun Yum (Goddess of Mercy); and on the far left is Shea Tan, dedicated to the local community, and housing several other gods.

Hong Kong Museum of History and Kowloon Park
The Hong Kong Museum of History stands in the middle of Kowloon Park, a green oasis in the heart of the city. There is a small permanent exhibition at the Museum outlining the history of Hong Kong before 1842.

Kowloon Park occupies the site of the former Whitfield Barracks, built by Major General Whitfield after the cession of the Kowloon Peninsula. On the north side of the park, parallel with Haiphong Road, military buildings house various government offices as well as the Hong Kong Archaeological Society.

Gun Club Hill Barracks, east of Tsim Sha Tsui, also dates from the 19th century and is still occupied by the British Army. The name 'Gun Club Hill' may originate either from a gun club based there, or from the firing ranges in King's Park which followed the present line of Wylie Road. The main entrance to the barracks was originally in Chatham Road.

Stonecutters Island
When Stonecutters Island was ceded to Britain in 1860 there were only a few fishermen and quarrymen living there, probably because the island lacked a supply of fresh water. Even today fresh water is delivered by boat.

The island was earmarked for defence works and used as a quarantine area but initially it served as a prison. Construction of the jail began in 1863 and was completed in 1866. However the crime rate subsided and it is thought it was hardly used. A severe typhoon in 1875 destroyed many of the buildings and all that remains today is a small chapel, a corner tower, a gate tower and a wall.

In 1871 the island was reserved as a quarantine area and smallpox cases were sent there, but there is only one grave on the island, that of Police Inspector W L Anningson (1845 - 1871). No traces remain of the lazaretto, a hospice for sufferers of contagious diseases including leprosy, which was constructed in the 1880s.

The first military buildings on the island were a gunpowder magazine and quarters for the officer-in-charge and his eight Chinese assistants built in 1870. In the mid-1880s construction of five batteries began and they were completed by 1899.

Stonecutters became a Naval Island in 1905 and was administered by the Royal Navy until 1957 when it was handed over to the Army. Between the wars the Navy built a huge armament depot, including 11 underground magazines. During the Japanese occupation of Hong Kong the island served as a rest and recreation centre for Japanese officers.

Soon to be incorporated in the development of the container port, Stonecutters is still a military area.

THE NEW TERRITORIES

Walled Villages

Tsang Tai Uk and Sheung Yiu are two outstanding examples of 19th-century walled villages in the New Territories. A third village, Hakka Wai, built a few years later in 1904–5, also merits inclusion in this section.

Construction of Tsang Tai Uk in the Sha Tin Valley was completed by the Tsang clan in 1850. The village has a thick, high surrounding wall with four corner towers, each with a metal trident protruding from the top, warding off evil spirits. The village is laid out in two rectangles, one inside the other, with a communal area in the centre.

By contrast, Sheung Yiu (meaning 'Above the Kiln') in Sai Kung is a very small, simple traditional Hakka village that, strictly speaking, is not walled. It stands on a high platform overlooking a river estuary and is naturally fortified. Entrance is through a gate tower that also once served as an observation post.

The villagers used to manufacture lime, bricks and tiles in addition to engaging in farming. Deserted 30 years ago, Sheung Yiu has been restored by the Regional Council and is now a folk museum. A lime-kiln near the village has also been preserved.

Hakka Wai at Sheung Shui was built by the Wong family who moved there at the beginning of the 20th century. The village comprises two rows of houses surrounded by a wall, with a school, library and ancestral hall. It is richly decorated, well maintained and has no disruptive modern buildings. Although it is not very old, it is one of the best walled villages in the New Territories.

Ancestral Halls

19th-century ancestral halls in the New Territories include the Pang Hall at Fanling, built in 1854, and Cheung Chun Yuen belonging to the Tang clan, constructed 120 years ago.

Both these halls are well maintained and in good condition. The Pang Hall in particular is one of the finest traditional buildings in the New Territories.

Study Libraries

Three particularly interesting study libraries in the New Territories date from the 19th century. Of these, the Kun

Ting study library at Ping Shan near Yuen Long is the best of its type in Hong Kong. This study library was built in the middle of the century by the Tangs, when the clan was at the height of its wealth and power. It commemorates a member of the 21st generation, Tan Kun Ting (1815 – 1838). Here the sons of the Tangs would study for the Imperial Civil Service examinations.

In 1987 the carved altar and part of the roof were destroyed by fire. The Jockey Club has donated $2 million to finance the restoration of this study library, one of the finest surviving in Hong Kong.

Close by are the remains of the Shut Hing study library, now demolished apart from its splendid entrance gate.

The third study library is at Fanling, the Sin Shut study library, and it also belongs to the Tangs. A date carved on the stone lintel above the entrance corresponds to 1840. It is in good condition although some of the original features have been repaired with modern materials.

Tai Fu Tai, Mandarin's House

Tai Fu Tai (meaning 'The Official's Residence') was built in 1865 at San Tin, Yuen Long, by Man Chung-luen, a prominent member of the Man clan. He was a successful merchant and a renowned philanthropist. The Qing emperor, Guangxu, bestowed on him the title 'Dai Fu' (*Tai Fu* in Cantonese).

Tai Fu Tai is a traditional Chinese official's residence; it is gracious, elegant and beautifully decorated with wood carvings, murals and delicate plaster mouldings. 19th-century Western influences are revealed in the painted-glass windows and baroque mouldings above the doorways. The ceramic figurines on the boat-shaped ridge of the roof were made at the Shiwan kilns in Guangdong.

Under the eaves of the main hall are two honorific boards dating from 1875 and engraved in both Chinese and Manchu, the only known examples in Hong Kong. Behind the walled compound of the house there is a grove of lychees.

In 1990 Tai Fu Tai was presented with the President Award by the Hong Kong Institute of Architects.

Hung Lau

Hung Lau (meaning 'The Red House') was probably built between 1885 and 1890 and was originally part of the Castle

89

The Mandarin's House, Tai Fu Tai, San Tin, New Territories, built in 1865

Peak Farm. It belonged to Li Kei-tong, a follower of Sun Yat-sen, and is reputed to have been a secret meeting place for Chinese revolutionaries.

Sun Yat-sen, father of modern China, is believed to have stayed at Hung Lau when he was a medical student in Hong Kong, graduating in 1892.

In a speech to students at the University of Hong Kong 30 years later, he said: 'The question I am often asked is where did I get my revolutionary and modern ideas: the answer is that I got my ideas in this very place, in the Colony of Hong Kong.'

Comparing the orderliness of Hong Kong with his home town in China, he said: 'There was disorder instead of order, insecurity instead of security...Afterwards I saw the outside world and began to wonder how it was that foreigners, that Englishmen could do such things as they had done, for example, with the barren rock of Hong Kong, within 70 or 80 years, while China in 4,000 years had no place like Hong Kong...Immediately after I graduated I saw that it was necessary to give up my profession of healing men and take up my part to cure my country.'

Kowloon Walled City
Until recently both Britain and China claimed jurisdiction over the notorious Kowloon Walled City, but neither government administered it. Now plans are in hand for the demolition of this historical enigma and the site will be made into a park.

The City is bounded by Tung Tau Tsuen Road and is instantly recognisable by the many illicit dentists' shops selling false teeth, which face onto the street. The alleys leading into the Walled City are dark, dripping and wet and dirty, and once inside it is very easy to get lost. Most people will find a look from the outside is sufficient to gain an impression of the interior. However the Walled City used to be a very different place.

A small fort was built on the present site by the Qing administration in 1810. In 1843, after Britain had taken over Hong Kong, a magistrate from San On county and a chief military officer of Dapeng county were transferred there and the garrison increased to 150 men.

It was soon felt that these measures were insufficient to 'constrain' the foreigners in Hong Kong and a wall was

Kowloon Walled City in 1927 (above); Cannon in Kowloon walled city, 1924 (below)

built in 1847 enclosing an area of 6.5 acres. It had six watchtowers, four gateways and embrasures for cannon. The wall was later extended up the hill to the north. A school was established in the City at the same time.

In 1847 the San On magistrate justifiably complained: 'In Kowloon the people mingle with foreigners and the custom of the residents is that they value money and material things and belittle poetry and studies.'

The Walled City served as a garrison town until the end of the century when it was incorporated into the New Territories. In 1898, the population of the garrison was 544 with 200 civilians, mainly soldiers' families. During the 19th century Europeans would go for walks and picnics on the mainland and the Walled City was a popular place of interest.

Most of the original buildings in the City were demolished as part of a 1930s slum-clearance scheme. Later, during the Japanese occupation the wall was used to provide material for the extension of Kai Tak airport.

After the Second World War, refugees from China crowded into the area and squatter huts gave way to high-rise buildings. The Governor, Sir Alexander Grantham, described the Walled City as 'a cesspool of iniquity, with heroin divans, brothels and everything unsavoury'.

All that remains of the 19th-century Kowloon Walled City is part of the former Yamen (Military office); two Chinese cannon; the inscribed lintel and doorframes of the old school; and a few stone inscriptions.

Lime-Kilns

Examples of traditional 19th-century lime kilns which have been preserved are at Sheung Yiu and Hoi Ha, both in Sai Kung.

Pak Sha O

Pak Sha O in Sai Kung country park, a remote multi-clan hamlet built in the 19th century, has been largely deserted by its former inhabitants. Today, many of the houses are let to people in the city as weekend homes.

One of the most interesting buildings is the ancestral hall of the Ho family. Richly decorated with murals, it is walled, stands on a platform, and has a watchtower. It is like a village within a village.

The tiny Roman Catholic Church was built in 1930.

Inscriptions

The Crane and Goose rock inscription is located behind the Hau Wong temple near Kowloon City. According to local tradition the characters for 'crane' and 'goose' were carved in 1888-9 by a famous scholar, Cheung Sau-yan, each one in a single movement without lifting his hand.

This is a remarkable feat given the complexity of the characters. Another poet added the couplets either side at a later date. The rock bearing the goose character was lost during the Second World War but there is a replica in the temple garden.

The Rain-Prayer Stone, erected in 1839 and dedicated to the god of rain and cloud is located on a hill near Sheung Shui. It was placed there by the Liu clan during a drought and ceremonies have been held from time to time during particularly dry seasons.

A FLOURISHING TRADING POST
THE EARLY 20TH CENTURY

With the signing of the Convention of Peking in 1898, British officials imagined there would be a smooth transition of power in the New Territories. However, as it turned out the handover was fraught with misunderstandings on the part of both the British and the Chinese governments.

Originally Hong Kong officials had wished to draw the northern boundary roughly where it is at present. The disadvantages of this demarcation were that the Chinese administrative unit of Shenzhen would be split in two, and it would be difficult to control cross-border smuggling. Stewart Lockhart, the Colonial Secretary, then suggested a border to the north of Shenzhen, but eventually a compromise was reached with the present boundary running down the middle of the main street in Sha Tau Kok.

The second bone of contention was that the treaty specified that a Chinese officer stationed within the Kowloon Walled City would continue to exercise jurisdiction unless it was inconsistent with the military requirements for the defence of Hong Kong. Officials in Hong Kong and Canton were completely at odds in their interpretation of this clause and the Chinese continued to regard the Walled City as part of their jurisdiction.

The third area of disagreement was the British demand that the Chinese customs stations in the New Territories collecting opium revenue, would be closed down.

With the delay in taking over the New Territories and growing unrest, the Governor, Sir Henry Blake, eventually decided in April 1899 that occupation should proceed regardless. He blamed the spontaneous opposition at Tai Po on the Viceroy of Canton who objected to the handover before full agreement had been reached on all points.

British troops moved into the New Territories and, after three days of desultory fighting, order was restored. The Kowloon Walled City was taken over and British soldiers moved into Shenzhen as well, although by September of that year they had withdrawn to the previously-agreed boundary. The Chinese customs posts were moved over the border and Kowloon Walled City remained an area of dispute.

The first tasks to be tackled by the British administration in the New Territories were construction of roads, police stations and district offices, followed by fortifications at Devil's Peak.

Entrepreneurs, including Sir Paul Chater, bought large tracts of land north of Kowloon and started building what would eventually be the garden suburb of Kowloon Tong. Sir Ho Kai and Au Tak, intent on creating a garden city, purchased land bordering on Kowloon Bay which they increased by reclamation and eventually sold to the Flying Club in 1929. It is now the site of Hong Kong International Airport, previously known as Kai Tak Airport.

Li Hung Chang (Governor General at Canton in 1900) and Hong Kong Governor Henry Blake (both seated)

On Hong Kong Island the Royal Navy decided to extend the dockyard and a graving dock was built in 1902. The Central Reclamation Scheme, opened by the Duke of Connaught in 1904, was finished in 1907.

The tramline from Kennedy Town to Shau Kei Wan along the north shore of the Island was opened in 1904, and in the early years of the century the first motor cars were imported. By 1915 Deep Water Bay was accessible by car, by 1917 Repulse Bay too, and in 1918 one could drive as far as the village of Tai Tam.

In 1907 Sir Frederick Lugard became Governor of Hong Kong and, together with Sir Hormusjee Mody, was instrumental in establishing the University of Hong Kong. The foundation stone was laid in 1910 and the University opened its doors to 72 students in 1912.

The British section of the Kowloon–Canton Railway was completed in 1910 and the section from the border to Canton in 1912. The new Supreme Court Building was finished in 1912.

During the First World War, Britain and Japan were allies and Hong Kong was virtually by-passed by the conflict. Nonetheless many thousands of Chinese left for the mainland in fear.

In 1918 Hong Kong had troubles of her own. The incident known as the Gresson Street shooting occurred in January when a band of Chinese armed robbers, cornered in Wan Chai, slaughtered five policemen and wounded five more before being shot and captured themselves.

In the following months disastrous fires occurred in the Cheung Sha Wan shipyards as well as in the stands at Happy Valley race course, causing 600 deaths. An outbreak of cerebral-spinal meningitis in overcrowded parts of the city was an additional nightmare.

After the First World War, there were major changes in the balance of power in East Asia. The 1922 Washington Treaties limited the fleets of Great Britain, the United States and Japan to a 5:5:3 ratio. However, since most of the Japanese fleet was concentrated in the Pacific, Japan had the greatest strength in these waters.

The Pacific powers also agreed not to build further fortifications in territories east of the 110° meridian, an imaginary line running from north to south through Hainan Island and the west coast of Borneo. This agreement severely limited Hong Kong's strategic rôle.

Between the two world wars, China was ravaged by political upheavals and civil war. Japan took advantage of China's weakness and walked into Manchuria, setting up the puppet state of Manchukuo in 1932.

Hong Kong felt the impact of unrest in China with an influx of refugees. In 1921, the Colony's population was 625,166, by 1937 it had increased to 1,006,982, and in 1941 it had reached 1,639,000.

Apart from the General Strike in 1925, Hong Kong flourished between the wars, becoming one of the principal ports in the world. The ship-building and ship-repair industries, concentrated at Hung Hom in Kowloon and Taikoo Dockyard at Quarry Bay, grew steadily, as did the manufacturing and textile industries.

Further land reclamation was carried out in Wan Chai and at Sham Shui Po and Lai Chi Kok. The last stretch of the main road round the New Territories was completed in 1920. A road was built to Shek O in 1923 and by 1924 one could drive from Wong Nei Chong Gap to Repulse Bay.

The 1918 fire at the Happy Valley race course, in which 600 people died

Marjorie Angus, who grew up in Kowloon between the wars, recalls in her book, *Bamboo Connection*:

The Peak Hotel stood at the top of the Peak Tram station, looking down over Hong Kong and Aberdeen. After a walk round the Peak on a cold winter's afternoon it was lovely to go in, sit in the lounge with blazing fires burning at each end, have tea and hot buttered muffins and look at the wonderful view of the Harbour and Kowloon .... Next to the Peak Hotel was the Old Peak Hospital, both were badly shelled during the war and never rebuilt.

The Star Ferry used to be very small and only carried 150 people. No Europeans ever went second class and no Chinese coolies were allowed in first class .... The Yaumati Ferries only started in a small way after 1924 and as far as I can remember there were no public ferries running to any islands except to Cheung Chau. All the big Hongs and firms had their own launches and there were a few public ones you could hire.

Kowloon was a lovely peaceful place when I first arrived here. No lorries, a few small buses that took fourteen people, only twelve private cars, and a few public ones you could hire for $3 an

An advertisement for the Sincere department store, c 1900, still one of the most successful Chinese-owned enterprises in Hong Kong (left); porcelain has always been a major Chinese product, as this magnificent display in the 'Yuk Chong' porcelain shop in Hong Kong, 1870, reveals (right)

hour. Nathan Road, from Salisbury Road up to Jordan Road (where the residential part of Kowloon in the mid-1920s finished) was lined with big trees on both sides. The road ran on to Mongkok with paddy fields on each side and the sea was quite near. The only buildings were the Police Station at Mongkok and a row of houses called Oriental Terrace.

Kowloon was very flat up to Austin Road, so we had no sedan chairs on this side, but as soon as you came off the Star Ferry on Hong Kong there was a row of these chairs waiting for you as well as a line of rickshaws.

There were large Chinese stores like Wing On, Sincere and Sun Company to shop in but they were in Hong Kong. And there were big Indian silk shops in Queen's Road, Chinese gold and silver shops and of course smaller shops selling Chinese curios. Foreign shops like Kelly and Walsh, Anderson's Music Store, Powell's men's shop, Lane Crawford and Whiteways were in Central. Most of the doctors had their offices in Central as did the steamship companies like Jardine, Butterfield and Swire, P & O and the American companies.

The gracious Peninsula Hotel opened for business in 1929. Marjorie Angus recollects:

There were no shops that I can remember in the Peninsula Hotel except Beten's Beauty Salon where the first permanent waves were given. I remember you could go there at 9 am and stagger home at 5 pm — a complete wreck after having your hair "permed" and a "perm" only cost $7.

In many ways the Second World War began for Hong Kong in 1937 when the Japanese attacked Peking and later, Shanghai. Thousands of refugees poured into the Colony and camps were set up on the Island, in Kowloon and throughout the New Territories. In 1938 the Japanese took Canton and closed the Pearl River to trade.

Britain was conscious of the Japanese threat to Hong Kong as early as 1933 when the Washington Naval Limitation Treaties were abandoned in the face of unacceptable Japanese demands. It was recognised that Hong Kong was in a tactically hopeless situation.

On 7 January 1941 Winston Churchill wrote to General Ismay: 'If Japan goes to war with us there is not the slightest chance of holding Hong Kong or relieving it.' Therefore a plan of defence was drawn up based on holding the Island and enough of the the mainland to protect the harbour for as long as possible.

Heavy artillery was stationed on the Island's southern coast and a line of pill-boxes, called Gindrinkers Line, was built from Gindrinkers Bay in the western New Territories to Port Shelter in the east against attack from the north.

The defence plan was amended in 1938 as by this time the Japanese were already close to Hong Kong. It was decided that since Kowloon and the New Territories could not be defended with the limited forces available, all troops would withdraw to the Island on the outbreak of war.

The barracks erected at Stanley a century earlier were in ruins. New barracks were built and 9.2-inch guns were sited at the end of the Stanley peninsula and at Cape D'Aguilar. These guns had been removed from Devil's Peak and Mount Davis.

Three 9.2-inch guns were retained at Mount Davis and 6-inch guns were mounted at Chung Hom Kok, Jubilee (further down Mount Davis) and Cape Collinson in addition to those already located at Lyemun and Stonecutters. More barrack blocks were built at Lyemun.

In July 1939, conscription for British subjects was introduced in Hong Kong. The Hong Kong Volunteer Defence Corps was strengthened and a Chinese Volunteer force was formed. In June 1940, amidst a storm of criticism, British women and children were evacuated from the Colony.

Sadly, all these preparations were in vain. On Monday, 8 December 1941, the Japanese attacked Hong Kong from the north. 36 fighters and 12 bombers destroyed the aeroplanes at Kai Tak in five minutes.

Japanese officers of the three regiments crossing the border at Shenzhen each carried a detailed plan of British defence positions. The pre-war Japanese intelligence network of waiters, barbers and masseurs in Hong Kong's hotels and clubs had done its work well.

One of the most tragic aspects of the fall of Hong Kong was the rôle played by the two battalions of the Royal Rifles of Canada and the Winnipeg Grenadiers. These troops, many of them raw recruits, were sent to Hong Kong at the eleventh hour, arriving in November 1941, in order to prolong resistance to the Japanese and boost the morale of the Hong Kong garrison. Many were to lose their lives in a theatre of war in which Canada had no direct interest.

When General Maltby heard about the Canadian reinforcements he changed the plan of defence back to the pre-1938 scheme. Gindrinkers Line was manned by the 2nd Royal Scots, the 2/14 Punjabis and the 5/7 Rajputs, supported by the Hong Kong and Singapore Royal Artillery; and Hong Kong Island was defended by the two Canadian battalions, the 1st Middlesex Regiment and the Hong Kong Volunteers.

Within five days the Japanese had occupied the New Territories and the Allied forces had withdrawn to the Island. On 13 December the Governor, Sir Mark Young, rejected Japanese demands to surrender and the Japanese began systematic shelling of military targets. Four days later, after continuous bombardment, the Governor was again asked to surrender and again he refused. On the night of 18 December the Japanese began their assault on the Island.

Six battalions landed on Hong Kong Island in two waves and proceeded to take the high ground. By dawn on 19 December the Japanese had gained control of the eastern

Rear Admiral C H J Harcourt receiving the Japanese surrender at Government House, September 1945

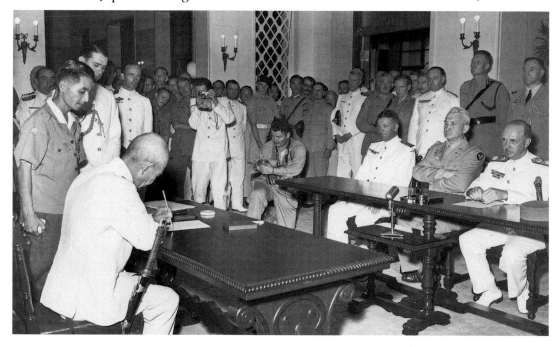

103

half of the Island. British, Chinese, Canadian and Indian soldiers were manning the coastal batteries around the Island. For three days while battle raged, the Repulse Bay Hotel, with 150 civilians — mainly women and children — was beseiged. On the morning of Christmas Eve 1941 the men, women and children were captured and marched off to internment at North Point.

On 23 December the Prime Minister, Winston Churchill, sent a message of encouragement to the beleaguered island but it was to no avail. By the afternoon of Christmas Day it was clear that military resistance was no longer possible and at 3.15 pm the Governor took the decision to surrender.

In his six-volume work *The Second World War*, Churchill praised Hong Kong's stand against the invading forces: 'On Christmas Day the limit of endurance was reached and capitulation became inevitable. Under their resolute Governor, Sir Mark Young, the Colony had fought a good fight. They had won indeed the 'lasting honour' which is their due.'

After the surrender prisoners of war were interned at Sham Shui Po Barracks and enemy civilians were interned at Stanley. In the following months the prisoners were re-organised so that the officers were housed at Argyle Street, the other ranks at Sham Shui Po and the Indians at Ma Tau Chung.

During the winter of 1942-3 overcrowding in the camps was relieved when 3,000 men were sent to Japan as prisoner-of-war labour. Prisoners were also used for work on the extension of Kai Tak Airport. The Japanese urged Chinese people to return to the mainland in order to reduce the imports of food to the Colony and by the end of the war the population of Hong Kong was reduced to 600,000.

In the city, English street names were replaced by Japanese. Queen's Road became Nakameiji-dori; Des Voeux Road, Katorido-dori; the Gloucester Hotel became the Matsubara and the Peninsula, the Toa Hotel. The Roman Catholic Cathedral bells were melted down, St John's Cathedral was used as a social club and St Andrew's Church was used as a rice-distribution centre. Government House was remodelled according to Japanese tastes and was used by the Japanese governor, General Rensuke Isogai. The Hongkong and Shanghai Bank building (since replaced by Norman Foster's masterpiece) served as the headquarters of the Japanese civil administration.

Three and a half years later, on 14 August 1945, the Japanese accepted defeat and on 30 August 1945 ships from the British Pacific Fleet arrived in Hong Kong bringing the Japanese occupation to an end.

The first hoisting of the Union Jack in Stanley, after Liberation Day, September 1945

EARLY 20TH-CENTURY BUILDINGS

HONG KONG ISLAND

Peak Café

Dating from 1901, the Peak Café, opposite the upper terminus of the Peak tram, was originally constructed as a chair shelter for sedan chairs and bearers. It has been altered extensively in the past 90 years.

From 1947 to 1989 the building functioned as a simple and well-loved café. In 1989 it passed into new hands and was given a much-needed face-lift. Today, under new ownership, the building continues to house the Peak Café and is one of the best examples of successful conservation in Hong Kong.

Rather than redeveloping the site, the new owner opted to carry out the necessary modernisation with sensitivity, and the building continues to give pleasure to visitors and Peak residents alike.

Churches

Perhaps the two most interesting 20th-century Protestant churches on Hong Kong Island are the Hop Yat Church in Bonham Road and St Margaret Mary's Church in Happy Valley. The Hop Yat Church was founded by Dr James Legge, a Scottish missionary and sinologist, who arrived in Hong Kong in 1843.

Legge established the Union Church in Hollywood Road in 1844 with services in both English and Chinese. In 1926 the Chinese congregation, by now independent, moved to the new Hop Yat Church in Bonham Road. The cornerstone of the original church is embodied in the present neo-Gothic style building.

St Margaret Mary's Church was built in 1923 for the growing congregation in Happy Valley. It is Renaissance Classical in style, with Greek and Roman decorative elements.

The Roman Catholic Sacred Heart Canossian College Chapel dates from 1907, but the first group of Sisters of the Canossian Order arrived in Hong Kong in 1860. The most famous member of the Order in Hong Kong was Emily Bowring, youngest daughter of the fourth governor. When she became a nun in Hong Kong in 1862 she took the name Sister Aloysia. The chapel, inaugurated by the Bishop of Amoy, is Renaissance Classical in style.

The Church of Jesus Christ of Latter-day Saints, an elegant red-brick and granite building in Castle Road, was originally the home of Ho Kam-tong, a successful merchant who was the brother of Jardines comprador, Sir Robert Ho Tung.

Ohel Leah Synagogue

The Ohel Synagogue, built in 1902, is Colonial Sephardic in design. Named after their mother, Leah Elias Sassoon, it was given to Hong Kong's Jewish community, under a trust, by Sir Jacob Sassoon and his brothers. It is the only surviving synagogue in Hong Kong and China.

The historical core of the Jewish community in Hong Kong is Sephardic but religious practice is mainly Ashkenazic. Sir Matthew Nathan was Hong Kong's only governor of the Jewish faith. During his term of office (1904 -1907) he was Honorary President of the Ohel Leah Synagogue. Prominent Jewish families who have settled in Hong Kong include the Sassoons, the Kadoories, the Ezras, the Gubbays and the Belilios.

Jamia Mosque

Located below Robinson Road, the Ohel Leah Synagogue has survived recent attempts to demolish and rebuild it. Thanks to vigorous action by public-spirited members of the community and a ruling by the Chief Rabbi of the United Kingdom and Colonies, it now seems that the building's future is assured.

Jamia Mosque

The first Muslims to settle in Hong Kong in the 19th century were Lascar seamen from the Southern Philippines. They lived in the area now known as Lower Lascar Row.

Later, Muslim Punjabis came from India, joining the police, the army and the prison service and also working as watchmen and bank clerks.

The first mosque was built at No 30, Shelley Street, in 1890. In 1915 a much larger mosque was constructed on the same site by an Indian businessman and philanthropist from Bombay, HMH Essack Elias.

The mosque, with its characteristic green-and-white minaret, was renamed Jamia Masjid after the Second World War. Hong Kong now has more than 50,000 Muslims of many different nationalities. The largest mosque in Hong Kong, which is completely modern, is in Nathan Road in Kowloon.

Old Pathological Institute

Built in 1905, the old Pathological Institute was originally called the Bacteriological Institute. The children's playground next to it is the site of the outbreak of a plague epidemic in 1894. Here in Hong Kong, Yersin and Kitasato, working in the midst of the epidemic, identified the bubonic plague bacillus independently but almost simultaneously.

The first Government Bacteriologist, William Hunter, was appointed in 1905. At this time the main diseases identified in Hong Kong were bubonic plague, cholera, beriberi, tuberculosis and smallpox. William Hunter and his successors conducted post-mortems, prepared smallpox vaccines, established the connection between rats and the spread of plague, examined water supplies and conducted research into infectious diseases.

The role of the Hong Kong Government Bacteriologist is graphically described in W Somerset Maugham's powerful and controversial novel about Hong Kong, *The Painted Veil*. After the Second World War the name of the building was changed to the Pathological Institute.

Old British Military Hospital

The first permanent military hospital, D'Aguilar's Hospital, was built in 1844 in Queensway, close to the present Police Headquarters in Arsenal Street. It was superseded by the new British Military Hospital built in Borrett Road in 1906.

Constructed under the supervision of Major Brookes, the British Military Hospital (BMH) in Borrett Road was officially opened in 1907. A report in the *Hong Kong Telegraph* of 5 July 1906 described the hospital as 'a credit to the Colony, its designers and builders, and we could wish that some of our local institutions were as up-to-date as this War Office product'.

Until 1938 the BMH had a specially small ambulance to bring patients to the hospital since the access road from Peak Road was only 3 metres wide and Bowen Road was closed to traffic.

During the Second World War British and Allied wounded and later, sick prisoners of war, were concentrated at the hospital and treated by the staff as best they could. There were severe shortages of food, medical supplies, clothing and fuel.

The hospital was retained by the Japanese, who allowed it to be visited several times by teams from the International Red Cross in attempts to demonstrate their observance of the Geneva Convention.

After the war the BMH continued its work, and casualties from the Korean and the Vietnam Wars were treated here. The hospital was closed in 1967 when the new BMH was opened in King's Park, Kowloon. The building is currently occupied by several charitable associations.

Matilda Hospital

The Matilda Hospital was named after Matilda, wife of Granville Sharp, a financier who had lived in Hong Kong for more than forty years. When he died in 1899, Sharp left over HK$2 million in his will for the construction of a hospital at Mount Kellett.

He stipulated that the hospital should be for 'the poor, the helpless, the forsaken and for him who is alone and desolate' and that it should be reserved for British, American and European patients. The 1910 annual report states that during that year 136 patients of 22 different nationalities were admitted.

The original building, opened in 1907, was built of red brick and granite. In 1934 it was covered with white Shanghai marble plaster. The east and west wings have since been demolished but the main body of the old hospital is still in use. The maternity unit was opened in 1915.

After the Second World War the hospital was requisitioned, first by the Hong Kong Government and then by the Royal Army Medical Corps. In 1951 the Matilda Hospital resumed its original role, amalgamating with the War Memorial Hospital, and becoming the Matilda and War Memorial Hospital. Now patients of any nationality were admitted and fees were charged for private rooms.

The Grayburn Wing was erected in 1952 with funds given by the shipping magnate, Haakon J Wallem. It was named after Sir Vandeleur Grayburn, Chairman of the

Matilda Hospital and Chief Manager of the Hongkong and Shanghai Bank, who died in the prison camp at Stanley.

The Legislative Council Building

The old Supreme Court (now the Legislative Council Building) was formally opened in January 1912 by the Governor, Sir Frederick Lugard. The building was designed by Aston Webb and E Ingress Bell, the architects of the Victoria and Albert Museum, Admiralty Arch and the façade of Buckingham Palace in London.

The old Supreme Court, constructed of granite, is neo-classical in style with Ionic columns, arches and a balustrade surrounding the building. The pediment over the main entrance bears the Royal Arms and the figures of Mercy and Truth. Above the pediment stands the statue of Justice, the Greek goddess, Themis. The building is surmounted by a dome and four pinnacles. Pockmarks from strafing during the Second World War are visible on the columns near the members' entrance.

The building was used as the Supreme Court until 1983. In 1985, after internal structural conversions costing HK$36 million, it became the home of the Legislative Council.

Wan Chai Post Office

The site on which Wan Chai Post Office stands is thought to be near the 1841 waterfront, at least a kilometre inland from today's waterfront road.

The Post Office, built between 1912 and 1913, opened for business in 1915. It is the oldest post office in Hong Kong, having served the people of Wan Chai for more than 70 years.

Wan Chai Post Office is a small, charming, one-storey building whose existence provides a sense of continuity between life in Hong Kong at the turn of the century and Hong Kong today.

University of Hong Kong — Main Building

The College of Medicine, founded by the doctors Sir Patrick Manson and Sir James Cantlie in 1887, was the forerunner of the University of Hong Kong. Sun Yat-sen was its most famous student.

In 1907 the new Governor, Sir Frederick Lugard, floated the idea of establishing a university in Hong Kong. A

110

Parsee businessman, Hormusjee Mody, responded at once, attaching a time limit and various conditions to his generous offer to fund the proposed university. These conditions were eventually met and both the British and the Chinese governments made contributions to the building and endowmment of a new university for Hong Kong.

Sir Frederick Lugard, who was the first Chancellor, laid the foundation stone in 1910 and the Main Building was completed in 1912. Hormusjee Mody received a knighthood but he died before the new buildings were complete.

The grand, imposing Main Building, located between Bonham Road and Kotewall Road, is Renaissance in style with granite colonnades. It is crowned by a clock tower and has four internal courtyards.

University of Hong Kong — Old Senior Common Room

Built in the Renaissance style with a graceful dome, the old Senior Common Room was completed in 1919. At first it was used by the Students' Union.

The building served as an administration building from

A painting of Wan Chai Post Office by Brian Tilbrook, 1990

1952 to 74, but for the past 15 years it has functioned as a Senior Common Room. Since the completion of the new Senior Common Room it has been used as an additional catering outlet for staff and students.

University of Hong Kong — Old Halls
The Old Halls, at the end of Lyttelton Road, are the University's first halls of residence. Lugard Hall, named after the University's founder, Sir Frederick Lugard, was opened in 1913; Eliot Hall was named after the first Vice-Chancellor, Sir Charles Eliot, and was opened in 1914; and May Hall, named after the first Chancellor, Sir Henry May, was opened in 1915.

During the Japanese occupation, Lugard and Eliot Halls were used as a temporary hospital, with May Hall housing the hospital's staff. During typhoon Wanda in 1966, landslides caused the collapse of the eastern ends of Eliot and May Halls. Later, Lugard and Eliot Halls were merged and eventually, with the addition of two connecting staircases, all three buildings were combined into what is now known as Old Halls.

University of Hong Kong — Sports Pavilion
The oval sports pavilion was completed in 1916 with funds donated by Ho Kwong, the son of the second of the three generous Ho brothers, Ho Tung, Ho Fook and Ho Kam-tong.

In 1948 the pavilion was extended. Plans are now in hand for a new sports hall to be constructed on, or near, the site with funds donated by Stanley Ho, Ho Kwong's immensely successful son, whose studies at the University were interrupted by the Japanese occupation.

Fung Ping Shan Musuem
Fung Ping-shan donated funds for the construction of a library for the University of Hong Kong, which was opened in 1932. By 1964, having outgrown its premises, the library was moved to its present site.

The Fung Ping Shan building, overlooking Bonham Road, now houses the University Museum. Its collections include many important pieces donated by the Fung family.

In addition to its holdings of Chinese bronzes, ceramics and paintings, the Museum possesses the largest collection

Archways near the entrance to the Chapel, University Hall

of bronze Yuan-dynasty Nestorian crosses in the world.

St Stephen's Girls' College
St Stephen's Girls' College in Lyttelton Road was one of the first schools for girls established in Hong Kong. Many of its pupils continued their studies as undergraduates at the University of Hong Kong, which opened its doors to women students in 1921.

St Stephen's was originally located in Caine Road but the school buildings were damaged in an earthquake in 1917. In 1922 the Prince of Wales laid the foundation stone for a new building. It was completed in 1924 and opened by the Governor's wife, Lady Stubbs.

The Chinese community provided a large proportion of the funds for the establishment of the school. It is managed by the Church Missionary Society.

Old Commodore's House
Originally named Iddesleigh, the Old Commodore's House, located in Bowen Road, was built in 1915. A certain Mr O Eager lived in the house between 1935 and 1941 when it was requisitioned by the Japanese for use as a residence for the Japanese naval commander. On his departure he left behind a fine pair of naval binoculars.

After the Second World War the Royal Navy leased the house until 1947 and then bought it for use as the residence of the Commodore (Hong Kong). The Royal Navy handed the house back to the Hong Kong Government in the 1970s when the Prince of Wales Building in HMS Tamar was completed. The Captain-in-Charge now lives in a spacious flat at the top of the building that has disrespectfully been likened to an inverted gin bottle.

The old Dairy Farm building, Wyndam Street, early 1900s

Old Dairy Farm Building
The first main depot of the Dairy Farm Company was built at the junction of Wyndham Street and Lower Albert Road in 1892. The present buildings on the site, dating from 1913 and 1917, are colonial in style. They were used by Dairy Farm until 1981, when they were taken over by the Foreign Correspondents' Club and the Fringe Club.

The Foreign Correspondents' Club has renovated its new home with care and imagination. The interior of the building is an example of how colonial buildings can be used to enhance the urban environment and remind people in Hong Kong of the not-so-distant past.

The Helena May

The Helena May in Garden Road is a three-storey Edwardian classical revival building. It houses a private residential club for women.

Known affectionately as 'The Virgins' Retreat', the Helena May was established in 1916 as 'a hostel for working women of moderate means' at the instigation of the Governor's wife, Lady Helena May. It was constructed with funds provided by the philanthropists, Sir Ellis Kadoorie and Ho Kam-tong.

During the Second World War it was occupied by the Japanese, and the original library was lost. Shortly afterwards, it was used as the headquarters of the Royal Air Force before returning to its original role.

Chinese YMCA

The first Chinese Young Men's Christian Association was located in Des Voeux Road in 1901. Later it moved to Queen's Road Central before it acquired its own purpose-built premises in Bridges Street in 1912.

This building soon proved too small for the YMCA's needs and a new YMCA was built across the street in 1918. Its style includes both Chinese and Western design elements.

Pedder Building

No 12 Pedder Street, now known as Pedder Building, was built between 1923 and 1925. Its first recorded owner was a certain So Shek-chung but from about 1926 to 1951 it was the property of Ng Wah. Although it is situated in the heart of Central, little is known about the history of the building.

Wan Chai and Old Upper Levels Police Stations

The Wan Chai and Old Upper Levels police stations were built in 1932 and 1935, each replacing an earlier police station on the same site.

In 1935 the police station in Wan Chai stood on the waterfront (now nearly a quarter of a mile away), a vivid reminder of the extent of land reclamation in the harbour during the past 50 years. The Upper Levels police station, of 1930s Colonial design, now houses the Criminal Investigation Department.

The Helena May, 1916

114

Stanley Fort

The fort on the headland at Stanley was built in the 1930s on the site of a small village named Wong Ma Kok. The Royal Engineers began work on an access road in 1934 and by 1937 new barracks, soldiers' quarters, officers' quarters, school, church and brigade mess were complete.

A pier was built on the north-western part of the peninsula in order that heavy items such as gun-mountings could be transported to Stanley by water.

Lieutenant Shearer, describing the construction of Stanley Fort in the *Royal Engineers Journal*, wrote:

It was realised from the beginning that the site for the barracks around Wong Ma Kok would require considerable anti-malarial work; the fact being forced home by the grim reminders in the Old Military Cemetery.

Incidentally, the original inhabitants of Wong Ma Kok were directly responsible for some of the graves, as they were pirates as well as farmers and fishermen. Two of the headstones in the cemetery are those of a Corporal and a Private who 'died of an attack of Chinese Pirates', whilst escorting the pay round from Victoria in a sampan; and later the pirates beheaded a couple of officers on Slaughter Point in full view of the garrison. As a result of this episode, the troops assaulted the village and when we took over in 1935, there were only about eight houses still standing.

Shearer continued: *One of the most amazing things to a newcomer to Hong Kong is the apparently airy manner in which an engineer will say, "Oh, we'll just take the top off that hill and fill in the valley here." The newcomer is even more impressed when he sees it done.*

. . . Another cause of wonderment is the Chinese bamboo scaffolding. . . it was not until 1934 that a steel-workers' erection crane was seen at work on the new Hongkong and Shanghai Bank Building.

Shearer was, of course, referring to the old Bank building.

Stanley Fort is still occupied by the British army and it remains a closed military area.

Mount Davis

Between 1906 and 1911 the summit of Mount Davis was levelled for the construction of a fort covering the western approaches to Hong Kong.

The fort headquarters were sunk in the plateau and five 9.2-inch guns were installed in circular concrete barbettes, three near the summit and two lower down the hill. In the late 1930s two guns at the summit were removed and transferred to Stanley.

During the Japanese assault in 1941 the guns were turned to face the mainland. There was no protection from air attack. Mount Davis was heavily bombed and shelled, receiving a direct hit on the fort headquarters where 50 or more men were sheltering. Miraculously, the shell failed to detonate.

Today one can wander around the old ruined fort and look at the disused barbettes, now overgrown by lush tropical vegetation. The damage wrought by the non-exploding shell can still be clearly seen.

Central Market

Central Market stands on the site of the old Central Market building which was demolished in 1937. The new market was completed in 1939.

It is one of the few buildings in Hong Kong designed in the early international style of Walter Gropius and the Bauhaus, fashionable in the 1920s in the West. Its form is simple, mainly rectilinear, with curved corners and an open internal atrium.

Noonday Gun

The Noonday Gun was immortalised by the English playwright, Noel Coward, in his song, *Mad Dogs and Englishmen*:

The Noonday Gun at Causeway Bay

'In Hong Kong
They strike a gong
And fire off a noonday gun . . .'

However, local historians are divided about the origin of both the Noonday Gun and the legends attached to it.

Jardines maintain that the tradition of firing a noonday gun arose from an incident which took place in the early years of British rule. Based at East Point (now Causeway Bay) since 1841, Jardines used to hold stocks of ammunition and man their own battery against attack by pirates.

On one occasion, so the story goes, the usual salute was

fired as the taipan's ship sailed into the harbour and approached East Point. A naval ship, with the Senior Naval officer on board, was in the vicinity and, being new to Hong Kong, he had not heard of the practice. Jardines were ordered to cease firing such salutes and, as a punishment for their breach of etiquette, were told to use up their stocks of ammunition by firing a noonday gun as a time signal for Hong Kong.

Doubt has been cast on the truth of this legend by a report in the Hong Kong Daily Press of 3 January 1870, noting that the continuance of the noonday gun firing 'is due to the liberality of Mr Magniac of Messrs Jardine, Matheson & Co, who when the Hong Kong Government ceased to provide this small return for the heavy military contribution forwarded annually from this Colony, purchased a gun and had it fixed up at Messrs Jardine, where it is fired daily.'

The second area of disagreement centres on the gun itself. Everyone concurs that the current noonday gun does not, in fact, date from the 19th century. The Royal Navy gave Jardines a gun after the Second World War as theirs had been removed by the Japanese.

In 1960 residents in Causeway Bay complained about the noise made by the daily firings of the Jardines six-pounder so the company agreed to swop their gun with a smaller three-pounder belonging to the Marine Police. The Jardines Hotchkiss No 6174 six-pounder, dating from 1918, can still be seen outside the Marine Police Headquarters in Kowloon.

It is the origin of the Marine Police three-pounder that is the subject of debate. The Police claim that the gun they gave to Jardines was mounted on Police Launch 4 in 1926. In 1946 the launch hit a mine and sank but the gun was rescued from the wreck. Eventually it was mounted on the lawn outside the Marine Police Headquarters.

Before this gun was given to Jardines it was refurbished by the Royal Navy in HMS Tamar. The Police claim that while in the dockyard, the block may have been changed.

Jardines have researched the history of their present gun and it appears that this gun, whose block is numbered 2008, dates from 1905 and saw service in HMS Southampton in the First World War and HMS Cardiff in the Second World War.

Perhaps the block, or the entire gun, was replaced while in HMS Tamar? The puzzle remains unsolved.

Boundary Stones

On Hong Kong Island six granite boundary stones, one-metre high, mark the perimeter of the City of Victoria. They were erected in 1903.

The ten-metre high obelisks north and south of Tai Tam Harbour are not, in fact, boundary stones. They are navigational markers erected by the Royal Navy at the turn of the century. The obelisks stand exactly 1.6 kilometres apart on the same line of longitude.

A third, much older set of milestones dates from the middle of the 19th century. They mark the distance, in each direction, to Stanley and the City of Victoria. They are inscribed in both English and Chinese. The Chinese name, Kwan Tai Lo, means 'apron string' and it refers to the old bridle path linking the early settlements.

KOWLOON
Churches

Completed in 1905, St Andrew's Church in Nathan Road is the oldest Protestant Church in Kowloon. The foundation stone was laid the previous year by Bishop Hoare.

St Andrew's was built with funds donated by the philanthropist, Sir Paul Chater, who was an Armenian Christian by birth. With a single bell tower, flying buttresses, stained-glass and marble columns, the church's design is Gothic with some Byzantine elements.

Chater also donated the vicarage next door, which was constructed in 1909. During the Second World War the Japanese used St Andrew's as a Shinto shrine.

The oldest Roman Catholic church in Kowloon is Rosary Church in Chatham Road South, built in 1905. It is Gothic in style with two towers at the front and one at the rear, and external buttresses.

In the 1920s two further Protestant churches were constructed: All Saints in Yim Po Fong Street, and Mongkok Church. In the 1930s a further two (Kowloon Union Church and Holy Trinity Church in Ma Tau Chung Road) were built, as well as the Roman Catholic church, St Teresa's, in Prince Edward Road.

118

Old Kowloon British School
The Kowloon British School, the forerunner of today's King
George V School in Kowloon Tong, was built in 1902 with
funds donated by Sir Robert Ho Tung. Designed by local
architects, Palmer and Turner, it is Neo-Gothic in style.

The building was planned as a primary school for about
60 English-speaking children. Later it expanded to include
secondary school children, catering for up to 200 in all. In
1936 the school was renamed the Central British School.

After the Second World War the building was used by
the Family Welfare Association and, from 1957, the Tsim
Sha Tsui Kaifong Welfare Association. This organisation is
now moving into new premises and, with renovation, the
old school will provide a fitting home for the Hong Kong
Government's Antiquities and Monuments Office.

Old Kowloon – Canton Railway Terminus Clock Tower
The 44-metre Clock Tower standing outside the new
Cultural Centre on the Tsim Sha Tsui waterfront belongs to
the old Kowloon–Canton Railway Terminus. The terminus
was completed in 1915 and opened to the public in 1916.
The Hong Kong section of the railway had been open to
traffic since 1910.

Although the Clock Tower was finished in 1915, the
installation of the electric turret clock and the one-ton hour
bell was delayed until 1921. The clock first told the correct
time on 22 March 1921. It remained out of order during the
Japanese occupation but it was restarted on 2 October 1945.

Originally the clock ran on batteries, but because
maintenance was difficult, four motors were installed, one
for each face. Unfortunately this resulted in the times
shown on each face all being slightly different and, because
they could not be synchronised, the use of the bell was
discontinued in 1950.

The Kowloon – Canton Railway Terminus moved to
Hung Hom in 1975 and the old building was demolished,
making way for the Urban Council's new Cultural Centre.
Many people were distressed and angry about the
destruction of one of Hong Kong's landmarks, and the
Governor finally ordered that the Clock Tower should be
retained.

The bell is currently on display in the concourse of Sha
Tin station whilst six granite columns from the old terminus

have been re-erected in an Urban Council park in Tsim Sha Tsui East.

Kowloon Police Stations
The police station at Yau Ma Tei was built in 1922, replacing an older station on the same site. In 1925 Sham Shui Po also had a new police station, and the same year, Kowloon Police Headquarters was constructed.

The headquarters building was not occupied until May 1932 when it became the Police Training School. Later it was used as a headquarters and, more recently, it has become part of the Mong Kok Police Station complex. The old Kowloon Police Headquarters' most recent claim to fame is its role in the BBC television programme about the Royal Hong Kong Police, *Yellowthread Street*.

Peninsula Hotel
In 1921, noting that there was a shortage of first-class accommodation for travellers in Kowloon, the Legislative Council proposed that a hotel should be built there. The Government approached the Hong Kong Hotel Company and in 1921 they unveiled plans to erect a HK$2 million hotel on the tip of Kowloon Peninsula.

Construction began in 1924 and the hotel was completed in 1927, whereupon it was immediately requisitioned as temporary accommodation for British troops. In 1928 the hotel was handed back to the owners, now named the Hong Kong and Shanghai Hotels Company.

On 11 December 1928 the hotel opened for business and immediately became a focal point of Hong Kong's social life.

After the fall of Hong Kong in 1941 the Governor, Sir Mark Young, and General Maltby crossed from Hong Kong Island to the Peninsula Hotel and formally surrendered the Colony to the commander of the Japanese army, Lieutenant General Sakai. Renamed the Toa Hotel, the Peninsula became the headquarters of the Japanese governor, Lieutenant General Rensuke Isogai.

After the Japanese surrender in 1945, the hotel was returned to the Hong Kong and Shanghai Hotels Company but it was requisitioned again, this time for offices and quarters for civil servants and prisoners-of-war. In June 1946 the Peninsula Hotel opened for business once more.

The Kowloon–Canton Railway Terminus Clock Tower, Tsim Sha Tsui

The hotel underwent a massive renovation in 1960 and in 1967 air-conditioning was installed throughout. The original fountain was replaced and a ballroom and discotheque were added. In 1969, at a cost of HK$7 million, service flats were converted into what is now the 120-room East Wing. In 1977, at a cost of HK$8 million, an additional shopping area was created.

The Peninsula Hotel continues to be an important landmark in Kowloon, being one of the very few pre-war buildings in Tsim Sha Tsui that have survived the ravages of time and developers.

Tung Wah Museum

The Tung Wah Museum, standing in the grounds of the Kwong Wah Hospital in Waterloo Road, was completed in 1911. Built at a cost of HK$140 million, the Kwong Wah was Kowloon's first hospital. However, the original hospital buildings have all been replaced except for the impressive Old Main Hall, which now houses the Museum.

The Peninsula Hotel, Kowloon, early 1950s

The Museum is a fine example of traditional Chinese architecture. It contains documents, photographs and memorabilia of the Tung Wah Group of Hospitals, an important and influential Hong Kong institution that has contributed enormously to the well-being of Hong Kong people during the past 120 years.

The Committee of the Tung Wah group of hospitals, 1888

The museum can be visited by arrangement with the Public Relations Department of the Tung Wah Group of Hospitals.

THE NEW TERRITORIES
Devil's Peak

The fort at Devil's Peak, situated north of the village of Lei Yue Mun in the New Territories, was built by the 40th Company, Royal Engineers and completed in 1914. The rocky outcrop upon which it was constructed was incorporated into the fort's design.

Originally the fort, which was an infantry position, had three 9.2-inch guns, two of which were located at Pottinger battery to the south. The third, known as Gough gun, was located just below the main fort and there was a 6-inch gun in support.

The gunners who manned the fort at Devil's Peak were stationed at Lyemun and ferried across the Strait. They did not see action during the First World War as Hong Kong was not a theatre of war. In the late 1930s the three 9.2-inch guns were transferred to Stanley and Cape D'Aguilar.

Two companies of Indian Army Rajputs were stationed briefly at Devil's Peak in 1941 but, following General Maltby's decision to pull back his troops to Hong Kong Island when the Japanese invaded the New Territories, they withdrew on 12/13 December 1941. Today the fort is in ruins.

Police Stations in the New Territories
When the unruly New Territories were taken over by Britain in 1898, one of the first tasks undertaken by the new administration was the provision of police stations.

The first police headquarters in the New Territories was built at Tai Po in 1899. It is now a divisional station soon to be superseded by new quarters currently under construction. The old police station at Ping Shan, also dating from 1899, was taken over by the station at Yuen Long in 1961 and it now provides a home for the Police Dog Unit.

The police stations at Tai O and Sheung Shui were built in 1902. Tai O continues to serve as a subdivisional station and Sheung Shui is now used as a Junior Police Call club house.

Cheung Chau and Lok Ma Chau police stations were constructed in 1913 and 1915 respectively, and they are now used as subdivisional stations, while Sha Tin and Ta Kwu Ling police stations were built between the wars, in 1924 and 1937. The old police station at Sha Tin is now the New Territories Regional Headquarters and Ta Kwu Ling is a divisional station.

Old Tai Po District Office
Following the take-over of the New Territories in 1898 the Hong Kong Government administered the region from offices at Tai Po. At first these offices consisted of a group of matsheds; later a building constructed in 1907 was destroyed by fire.

The old Tai Po District Office dates from 1910. Here the New Territories Administration planned the development of the region and its infrastructure, including the introduction of metalled roads, electricity and clean piped water to the villages.

Old Tai Po Market Railway Museum
The Old Tai Po Market Railway Museum is housed in a railway station built in 1913. The station's exterior is unique, as it resembles a Chinese temple. All the other stations on the British Section of the Kowloon – Canton railway were built to a standard design.

Inside, the old station has a central hall with two side wings. One wing served as staff quarters and the other contained a booking office, a signals cabin and an administration office.

In 1983 the station was replaced by a new one further down the line. Restored by the Regional Council, it contains displays of old rolling stock, ticket machines, uniforms,

The Hong Kong Railway Museum at the Old Tai Po Market station

signals and photographs. The building was declared a monument in 1984.

Island House, Tai Po

Island House at Tai Po was built in 1905 and is now the local headquarters of the World Wildlife Fund for Nature. Declared a monument in 1982, it was until recently the official residence of the District Officer, New Territories.

Island House is Colonial in design, constructed of red brick and finished in white plaster. It has open verandahs on the ground and first floors and a tower at one corner which used to contain a beacon to guide ships through the Tolo Channel.

Besides detached servants' quarters and stables, Island House has a superb garden with many interesting trees and shrubs. The World Wildlife Fund for Nature has a small information centre which is open to visitors.

Hoi Pa Village House

Hoi Pa was a Hakka village that served as a market for the Tsuen Wan area before being redeveloped in the 1950s. The house at Lot 917 in the former village of Hoi Pa belonged to a scholar named Yau Yuan-cheung (1865 – 1937).

Yau grew up in Tsuen Wan and had a traditional Chinese education. He failed the Imperial Examinations several times and left Hong Kong at the age of 20 to settle in Jamaica, working there for ten years as secretary to an overseas Chinese merchant association. While abroad Yau raised money amongst his compatriots for the construction of a Tin Hau temple in Tsuen Wan.

On his return to Hong Kong Yau built a house in Hoi Pa village. Completed in 1904 at a cost of HK$1,825.20, the house is beautifully decorated and of traditional Hakka design.

Yau was an active participant in local affairs and was greatly respected by his fellow villagers. His son, Yau Tung-hoi, donated Yau Yuan-cheung's collection of books and papers to the Government in 1982. The collection comprises 30 titles in 146 volumes together with 28 volumes of manuscripts and 90 loose leaves of Chinese poems and essays. The Government declared Hoi Pa village house a monument in 1986.

Pun Uk, Yuen Long

Pun Uk, a Hakka mansion in Yuen Long, was built by a Chinese entrepreneur, Pun Kwan-min, who made his fortune in Indonesia. Born in Mei Xian in northeast Guangdong, Pun was a Hakka who chose to settle in Hong Kong. He contributed large sums of money for the construction of Pok Oi Hospital in Yuen Long and for schools in his native home in Guangdong.

Pun Uk, still occupied by members of the Pun family, has six halls, 16 rooms and two internal courtyards, with an open courtyard and a fish-pond in front of the house. It is decorated with carved wooden panels and murals.

In the 1930s Marshal Ye Jian-ying, one of the Communist Chinese leaders, was a guest in the house. During the Japanese occupation the house was used as the headquarters of the Japanese forces in Yuen Long.

Po Lin Monastery

In 1905 three reclusive monks established the Po Lin Buddhist monastery in a group of stone huts on Lantau. *Po Lin* means 'Precious Lotus', the lotus flower being the symbol of the Buddhist faith. The small community gradually increased in numbers and in 1927 the monastery was officially inaugurated.

The Po Lin Monastery was housed in a group of simple buildings until the late 1960s, when two more temples and two pavilions were constructed from donations totalling HK$2 million. The new buildings were opened in 1970. The monastery's original temple is still used by the monks and nuns, who pray there twice a day.

Nowadays the Po Lin Monastery is a large and thriving community, receiving thousands of visitors every week. Its most recent marvel is the massive and magnificent bronze statue of Buddha gazing out to sea. Constructed by engineers from the People's Republic of China, at 22 metres high it is the largest outdoor bronze statue of Buddha in Southeast Asia.

Tao Fong Shan Christian Centre

The Tao Fong Shan Christian Centre, standing on a peaceful wooded hill above Shatin, was founded by the Norwegian missionary, Dr Karl Ludvig Reichelt, in 1931. Reichelt's calling was to undertake missionary work amongst the

*Views of Po Lin Monastery complex
Lantau*

Buddhists in China. At the Tao Fong Centre he and his colleagues organised courses in Christianity for Buddhist monks.

The unusual octagonal Christ Temple was designed by Johannes Prip-Moller, a Dane who specialised in Chinese Buddhist architecture. The building was constructed in such a way as to make Buddhist monks feel comfortable in Christian surroundings.

The ornate Chinese altar has a Christian cross, but it is depicted rising from a lotus, a traditional Buddhist emblem. Completed in 1934, the simple chapel/meditation hall was originally furnished with floor cushions rather than pews.

The rest of the buildings, of traditional Chinese design, were completed in the 1930s. The Institute also has a porcelain workshop.

Shing Mun Redoubt

Gindrinkers Line was the name given to a string of trenches, pill-boxes and bunkers constructed before the Second World War across the hills to the north of the Kowloon Peninsula, from Gindrinkers Bay in the west to Port Shelter in the east.

As with the Maginot Line of the First World War in Europe, army commanders thought that Gindrinkers Line was impregnable but, sadly, the Japanese attack in 1941 proved its defensive capability to be illusory.

Forming a key part of Gindrinkers Line, the Shing Mun redoubt was a 12-acre mini-citadel situated underground on the northern part of Smugglers' Ridge, guarding the most vulnerable land route to Kowloon.

Each of the tunnels in the network was named after a street in London. It was designed to enable 120 men to last out for 14 days without reinforcement. However, when the redoubt was defended in earnest in 1941, it was manned by only 30 men, mainly from the Royal Scots Regiment.

Japanese troops, commanded by Colonel Doi, made a surprise attack on the redoubt on the night of 9 December 1941. Undetected, 150 men scaled Smugglers' Ridge in the early part of the night and at 11 pm they descended on the redoubt, throwing hand grenades down the ventilation shafts.

The main force then attacked from the direction of the reservoir. By morning, after five hours of fierce fighting, the redoubt was taken. Gindrinkers Line had been breached and Kowloon was open to attack. It was only a matter of days before the Japanese took over the whole of the Kowloon Peninsula.

Although the tunnels and pill-boxes are scarred, dilapidated and overgrown the system has largely survived the ravages of war and time. It is a poignant reminder of one of the turning points in Hong Kong's history.

Boundary Stones
There are boundary stones on the islands of Lantau and Cheung Chau and also running down the middle of the border village of Sha Tau Kok.

On Lantau two stones are located just east of Tai O and Fan Lau, marking the sea boundary with China. Dated 1902, they are inscribed in English and Chinese, and were erected by Lieutenant Commander F M Leake, Royal Navy, and the officers of HMS Bramble.

On Cheung Chau six boundary stones dating from 1919 mark the area in the southern part of the island where residents once had to obtain permission from the Governor if they wished to live there.

The eight boundary stones in Sha Tau Kok stand in the middle of Zhong Ying Street, marking the legal frontier of Hong Kong and China. They are inscribed in English 'Anglo—Chinese Boundary 1899' and also in Chinese. Sha Tau Kok is a closed area and permission must be obtained if you wish to visit this village.

THE ECONOMIC MIRACLE
HONG KONG SINCE WORLD WAR II

The end of the Japanese occupation in 1945 found Hong Kong in a sorry state. Food and fuel were in short supply and rice was rationed. But it was not long before the resilient Hong Kong people began to get back on their feet. Hotels were requisitioned to cope with the lack of accommodation, and repairs were made to war-damaged property. Lorries were converted for use as buses and somehow the utilities were kept running, or re-started, in many cases with the help of the armed services.

Together with improvements in living conditions there were changes in the political system, but alterations to the constitution over the next decade were fairly limited. Although proposals by the Governor, Sir Mark Young, to introduce democracy were shelved, by the late 1950s Hong Kong had become, administratively and financially, virtually autonomous.

The most important change was the emergence of a powerful Chinese élite able to compete with and challenge British merchants and officials in all spheres of public life. Chinese firms came to dominate many aspects of commerce and industry; Chinese lawyers were appointed to the judiciary and Chinese were accepted into the administrative grades of the Civil Service.

At the same time the huge influx of refugees from China, both immediately after the war and then in the early 1950s escaping from the new Chinese Communist régime, put Hong Kong under immense social and economic pressure, stretching the Colony's incipient social services to their limit. At the end of 1946 the population was 1.6 million; by 1956 it had grown to 2.5 million. New government departments, such as Social Welfare, Resettlement, Immigration, Statistics and Planning, Labour and Mines, and Government Information Services, were created to deal with the multitude of problems caused by the rapid growth in population.

The terrible fire which broke out amongst squatter huts at Shek Kip Mei on Christmas Day 1953, when 50,000 people lost their homes, was the final factor forcing the Government to embark on an ambitious programme of rehousing and slum clearance. The first resettlement estates were basic and built to minimum acceptable standards; later resettlement estates provided more comfortable accommodation. By the end of 1970 the Government had rehoused more than one million people.

None of this could have been foreseen in the early 1950s. Hong Kong's economy was suffering from the effects of the closed border with China during the Chinese Civil War

A Chinese bazaar in the early 20th century

133

The terrible fire at Shek Kip Mei, 25 December 1953 (top left); some of the squatter areas and the temporary housing erected after the Shek Kip Mei fire (bottom left); the construction of one of the resettlement estates (right)

(1946-1949), and from sanctions imposed against China following the Korean War (1950-53). Denied its past rôle as an entrepôt for China, the territory responded by becoming a manufacturing centre in its own right, but it was to be a long, slow haul.

Incoming refugees provided the workforce that helped to create Hong Kong's spectacular post-war growth. From Shanghai, in particular, came talented entrepreneurs and skilled workers, bringing capital and industrial expertise. By 1963 exports had recovered to exceed their 1951 level, and three-quarters of Hong Kong's exports were domestic exports rather than re-exports. Hong Kong was now a manufacturer of textiles, enamelware and plastic and rubber goods, soon to be followed by the assembly of consumer electronics.

The economic boom of the early sixties faltered when Communist-inspired riots broke out in 1967, a manifestation of the turmoil of the Cultural Revolution and the activities of the Red Guards on the mainland.

During the summer of that year tension increased, and pro-Peking demonstrations were held outside Government House and in Central. In July, the Hong Kong Government assumed emergency powers to preserve law and order. Throughout the rest of the year there were sporadic disturbances, but Hong Kong weathered the worst of the storm and by the end of the following year peace had returned to the territory.

At the time of the Vietnam War, Wan Chai had developed

Making flashlight batteries, 1956

136

as a red-light district, its bars and dance-halls providing rest and relaxation for thousands of American servicemen. Today much of the old 'Suzie Wong' waterfront area has been redeveloped, but its notorious past lingers on in a few garish neon-lit streets.

1972 was a turning point for Hong Kong. The Vietnam War ended; a new governor, Sir Murray MacLehose, was appointed; and China turned her attention to cultivating closer diplomatic and economic ties with the West.

In his ten years as Governor (1972-1982), Sir Murray MacLehose (now Lord MacLehose) tackled two enduring and intractable problems — immigration and corruption — with a large measure of success. Part of this success can be attributed to China's new outward-looking foreign policy, resulting from President Nixon's initiative in China culminating in the 1972 Shanghai Communiqué.

MacLehose was able to persuade Peking to link the limitation of legal immigration from China to Hong Kong with a policy of Hong Kong returning to the mainland illegal immigrants caught crossing the border. Since the beginning of the 1970s, when the population was around four million, British soldiers and the Royal Hong Kong Police intercepted illegal immigrants at the border and sent them back to China. Nevertheless huge numbers continued to reach Hong Kong, swelling the population to five million by the beginning of the 1980s.

In 1973 the Housing Department prepared plans for the construction of three 'first-generation' new towns in the New Territories — Tsuen Wan, Sha Tin and Tuen Mun — to accommodate the ever-increasing population. By the 1980s three 'second-generation' new towns were built, at Tai Po, Sheung Shui and Yuen Long. The programme continues today with two further townships being created, at Junk Bay and Tin Shui Wai. At the end of 1989 Hong Kong's population stood at 5.8 million.

MacLehose will also be remembered for his onslaught against the corruption that was endemic in the police and public services. The Independent Commission against Corruption (ICAC) was established in 1974 under the leadership of Sir Jack Cater and its investigations were far-reaching. Thanks to the work of the ICAC, ethical standards in the public services, the professions and commerce have improved markedly.

Star Ferry fare increases set off a string of riots, April 1966

137

From 1975 onwards, after the conquest of South Vietnam by the North, refugees flooded out of the ravished and impoverished country. Many were ethnic Chinese who had settled in the cities of South Vietnam. Faced with the prospect of being sent to the countryside to work in the paddy fields, they risked their lives by heading for Hong Kong in small, unseaworthy boats. Many died on the journey, running out of fuel and food, being attacked by pirates or drowned in typhoons. Ethnic Chinese were also being expelled from north Vietnam across the border into China.

Hong Kong responded nobly and housed the refugees in open camps while they waited to be resettled in third countries. In 1982 some Vietnamese boat people were moved into closed camps from which they could not go out to work.

The situation worsened considerably in 1989 when 34,000 Vietnamese boat people arrived in Hong Kong. It was considered that many were not deserving of refugee status, that is they were not under threat of persecution in their own country, but were economic migrants seeking a better life. From June 1988 Vietnamese boat people have been screened by the Hong Kong Immigration Department, working closely with the United Nations High Comissioner

Catching illegal immigrants, 1982

K GOVERNMENT TO PERMIT US TO LAND AT ONCE

請求港府以人道精神解決我們早日上

Vietnamese boat people arriving in Hong Kong, late 1970s

for Refugees, to determine which of them are genuine refugees. Those not granted refugee status have been held in detention centres pending repatriation to Vietnam.

The boat people have suffered many privations and frustrations but the economic burden has been borne by the people of Hong Kong. The cost in 1989 was HK$471 million.

During the past twenty years the rate of infrastructural development in the private sector has been impressive. Huge acreages of land have been reclaimed from the sea, power stations have been built, reservoirs constructed and telecommunications developed. In the 1980s Hong Kong's container port at Kwai Chung became the busiest in the world.

Most Hong Kong people would probably agree that their lives have been affected above all by changes in the territory's transport systems. Two underwater road tunnels now traverse the harbour; the Mass Transit Railway, the Kowloon–Canton Railway and the Light Rail Transit take millions of workers to offices and factories every day;

Sha Tin, one of the 'first-generation' new towns in the New Territories

tunnels have been bored through the hills of Kowloon and Hong Kong Island for cars and lorries, and high-speed ferries carry passengers to Macau and Guanzhou. In the business districts of Hong Kong Island and Kowloon smart office blocks and adventurous public buildings have been designed by some of the world's leading architects.

Much of Hong Kong's physical development has been brought about by the opening of China to the West in the 1970s when Hong Kong once again became a major conduit of trade with China. However, this time there was a difference: China now imported goods directly from Hong Kong as well as buying re-exports from the rest of the world. The $1.6 billion worth of direct imports from Hong Kong in 1980 had grown to $15 billion by 1985, and the value increases each year. China is Hong Kong's biggest trading partner, accounting for about a quarter of the territory's total exports and imports.

During the 1980s, Hong Kong has also become a giant 'department store' for China. Here the People's Republic of China has been able to acquire foreign goods and services and absorb new ideas and technologies in addition to observing them in operation in the territory.

In 1982, Sir Edward Youde was appointed Governor of

140

Hong Kong. During his brief term of office before his untimely death in 1986, he was to be involved in the negotiations over the termination of the lease of the New Territories in 1997.

The British Prime Minister, Mrs Thatcher, visited Beijing in September 1982, for private talks, and during this visit she stated that Britain had a moral responsbility and duty to the people of Hong Kong. She shared a justified pride in their achievements in the territory. The government of the People's Republic of China, however, made it clear that the resumption of sovereignty over the territory of Hong Kong in 1997 was not negotiable.

People who had fled from the mainland and those who had grown up in the territory (more than half the population) were uneasy. Despite its many drawbacks, *laissez-faire* colonial rule by the British with its many freedoms — not least of which was the freedom to engage in free enterprise — seemed preferable to that of the Chinese Communist Party. Hong Kong's Western lifestyle seemed to be in jeopardy.

In the months following Mrs Thatcher's Beijing visit, while talks continued in secret between the British and Chinese governments, the Chinese leader, Deng Xiaoping, attempted to allay fears in Hong Kong by advocating that Hong Kong people should rule Hong Kong, coining the slogan 'one country, two systems' to describe the

Kwai Chung, the busiest container terminal in the world

141

relationship between China and Hong Kong; and the British emphasised the need to maintain 'stability and prosperity' in the territory. No-one really knew what the two governments had in mind until the Sino-British Joint Declaration on the question of Hong Kong was finally promulgated in 1984.

The Joint Declaration provides a statement of human rights, a declaration of aims, and a simple model of a new autonomous representative and democratic government to oversee the continuation of Hong Kong's present way of life for 50 years after 1997. British diplomats hailed it as a success, since Britain would be withdrawing from Hong Kong 'with honour'; and China was satisfied, as she would be regaining sovereignty over the territory.

Notwithstanding the promises made in the Joint Declaration and the proposed system of government outlined in the Basic Law, promulgated in 1990, increasing numbers of the more prosperous, talented professional people have chosen to seek a more certain future by emigrating to countries such as Australia, Canada and the United States.

In June 1989 mainland Chinese students demonstrated peacefully in Peking's Tiananmen Square against corruption and for democracy. The subsequent incident between the students and the People's Liberation Army on June 4 caused immense sorrow and alarm in Hong Kong. Before and after June 4, thousands of Hong Kong people demonstrated in solidarity with their compatriots on the mainland.

The prospect of the Communist Chinese leadership allowing full democracy to flourish in the territory either before or after 1997 appeared highly unlikely, as did the possibility of Hong Kong people retaining the human rights and freedoms guaranteed in the Joint Declaration. The growing stream of emigrants showed no signs of abating.

The Signing of the Joint Declaration in September 1984, by Sir Richard Evans, British Ambassador to Peking and Zhou Nan, leader of the Chinese delegation. Sir David Wilson is also pictured (above) British Prime Minister Margaret Thatcher's historic meeting with Deng Xiaoping, the Chinese Premier, 1982 (below)

In Hong Kong many felt that during the preceding five years some of the principles of the Joint Declaration had already been eroded by the People's Republic, and that now was the time for it to be renegotiated.

There were many suggestions, but the immediate answer, provided by the British government, was to give 50,000 full British passports to heads of households of key people in

142

government, industry and the professions in order that they should feel secure in Hong Kong until 1997 and beyond, safe in the knowledge that they could emigrate at any time. Whether this measure will in fact anchor people in Hong Kong and provide confidence in the future of the territory remains to be seen.

In the autumn of 1989 the Hong Kong Government announced plans for a massive HK$127 billion programme of infrastructural development — the Port and Airport Development Scheme — designed to strengthen Hong Kong's economic future. A new airport, capable of handling 80 million passengers a year, has been proposed for construction at Chek Lap Kok on the northern coast of Lantau Island. The port facilities will include new container and general cargo terminals, together with a supporting road and rail network.

After several years of discussion and consultation, the Basic Law of the future Hong Kong Special Administrative Region of the People's Republic of China was promulgated on 4 April 1990 at the Third Session of the National People's Congress in Peking. The Basic Law is the blueprint for the constitution of the territory after 1997.

The articles of the Basic Law uphold many of the rights and freedoms currently enjoyed by Hong Kong citizens, but the Law will be subordinate to the National People's Congress in Beijing. Strictly speaking, it is a statement of policy and intent rather than a constitution similar to that of the United States. However, the People's Republic of China has promised that the current social and economic systems in Hong Kong will remain unchanged for 50 years, and it is on this promise that the Hong Kong people rely.

Hong Kong is once again at a turning point in its history. As always, the territory will find its own way of riding out the storms and capitalising on the challenges ahead. Hong Kong is the home of six million people, of whom 98% are Chinese. They have created the world's eleventh largest trading economy. The territory is now the world's largest exporter of watches and clocks and the second largest exporter of garments. Hong Kong is arguably the most important trading centre of Southeast Asia.

Sadly, in many instances, Hong Kong's rapid economic growth has taken place at the expense of her historic buildings. Few still stand in the urban areas and many have

A pro-democracy rally in Hong Kong, 3 June 1990

been redeveloped. Casualties have included the old Hong Kong Club, Murray House (soon to be re-erected in Stanley) and the former Kowloon Canton Railway Terminus.

Hong Kong lags behind most other developed countries and territories in the conservation of her antiquities, but public concern about the quality of the urban environment is increasing. There is growing awareness that positive action is needed to preserve what remains of old Hong Kong.

Fortunately the outlook is optimistic. Plans are in hand to create a Heritage Trust so that historic buildings can be preserved and used to good effect, rather than demolished in favour of newer, bigger skyscrapers.

Hong Kong people have much to be proud of. The territory is unique — a monument to hard work, resourcefulness, tolerance and humanity. It is only fitting that care should be taken to preserve the material remains of the past in the midst of this great international city.

The former Supreme Court, now the Legislative Council, built on reclaimed land in 1912. The base of the Bank of China tower can be seen immediately behind

POST-WAR BUILDINGS

RESETTLEMENT ESTATES

Shek Kip Mei, the first resettlement estate, was built by the Hong Kong Government to rehouse the 50,000 people made homeless after their flimsy squatter huts were burnt down in 1953. Six-storey H-shaped concrete blocks, containing 384 rooms measuring just over 11 square metres, provided rudimentary accommodation. There were two standpipes and six flush lavatories for each floor. Shared communal facilities were located in a central area away from the living quarters.

During the 1950s the Government continued its building programme to rehouse squatters; and from around 1960 resettlement estate blocks were built to improved designs. These had enclosed courtyards and staircases, private balconies for each room, and four large ground floor shops. It was not until the advent of the Mark IV design in 1963 that tenants had lifts and self-contained units with private bathrooms and kitchens. Mark VI resettlement blocks, introduced in 1970, were altogether more spacious.

The Housing Authority has committed itself to redeveloping the early Mark I-IV estates by stages.

PUBLIC HOUSING ESTATES

Apart from low-cost resettlement estates for the homeless, during the 1950s the Government also built a better type of accommodation to help alleviate the housing shortage in the territory. The first public housing estate, at North Point, was completed in 1958. Each flat was self-contained with a separate bedroom, kitchen, bathroom and balcony.

Wah Fu Estate at Aberdeen, completed in 1967, was the eighth and largest estate developed so far by the Housing Authority. Consisting of 25 multi-storey blocks with flats of various sizes, it is a self-contained township with a shopping centre, car parks, public transport, schools, welfare centres and recreational areas. Wah Fu was used as a model for later housing estates.

The goal of the new Hong Kong Housing Authority, established in 1973, was to provide better housing for one and a half million people over a period of ten years. The Oi Man Estate in Ho Man Tin, Kowloon, was one of the first estates to be built by the Authority. A number of two-bedroom flats were included, together with the installation of a communal telelvision antenna system. From then on all housing estates had fully air-conditioned commercial centres with shopping arcades. Currently nearly two and a half million people live in public housing estates in Hong Kong and the New Territories.

Apart from rental accommodation, the Housing Authority also builds homes for private ownership under the Home Ownership and Private Sector Participation schemes. About a quarter of the 40,000 units produced annually are for private ownership.

NEW TOWNS

By 1973 it was clear that sufficient land was not available in the urban areas of Hong Kong and Kowloon to accommodate the planned new housing developments. The Housing Authority embarked on its New Town Programme in the New Territories. Tsuen Wan, Sha Tin and Tuen Mun were designated as the sites of these 'first-generation' new towns.

In order to provide further areas for urban development, plans were drawn up in 1979 for 'second-generation' new towns at Tai Po, Sheung Shui/Fanling and Yuen Long. Planning started on 'third generation' new towns at Junk Bay and Tin Shui Wai in 1982.

Private housing developments have flourished alongside public housing schemes. It is expected that about 60% of the total planned population in most new towns will live in high-rise, high-density, public rental housing estates.

Despite the best efforts of the architects and planners, the new towns are, inevitably, concrete jungles. They were built very quickly to accommodate huge numbers of people and in this respect they have fulfilled their purpose admirably. Although not always aesthetically pleasing, many of the towns are surrounded by green hills and, because most are located close to country parks, people can hike, barbecue and 'get away from it all' at weekends without too much difficulty.

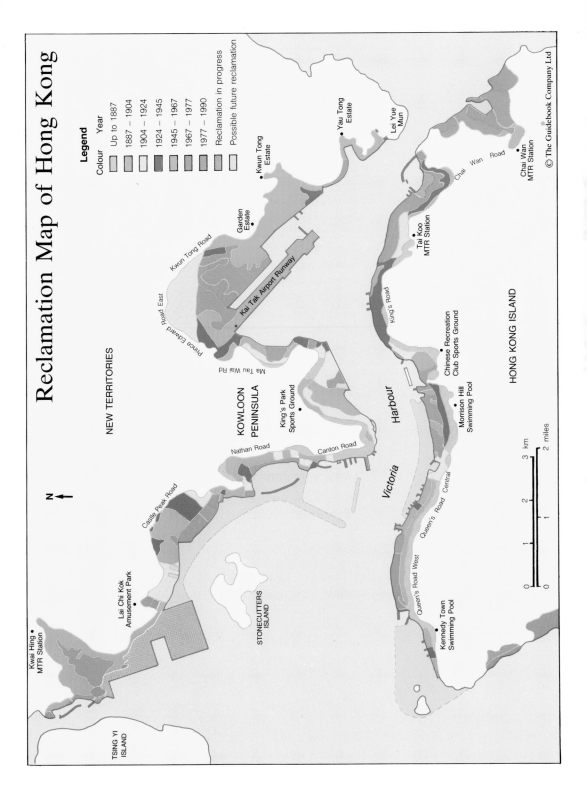

Reclamation Map of Hong Kong

Legend

Colour	Year
	Up to 1887
	1887 – 1904
	1904 – 1924
	1924 – 1945
	1945 – 1967
	1967 – 1977
	1977 – 1990
	Reclamation in progress
	Possible future reclamation

N

NEW TERRITORIES

TSING YI ISLAND

Kwai Hing ● MTR Station

Lai Chi Kok Amusement Park ●

Castle Peak Road

Nathan Road

Canton Road

KOWLOON PENINSULA

King's Park Sports Ground ●

Kwun Tong Road

Prince Edward Road East

Ma Tau Wai Rd

Kai Tak Airport Runway

Garden Estate ●

Kwun Tong Estate ●

Yau Tong Estate ●

Lei Yue Mun

STONECUTTERS ISLAND

Victoria Harbour

Queen's Road West

Queen's Road Central

Kennedy Town Swimming Pool ●

Morrison Hill Swimming Pool ●

Chinese Recreation Club Sports Ground ●

King's Road

Tai Koo MTR Station ●

Chai Wan Road

Chai Wan MTR Station ●

HONG KONG ISLAND

0   1   2   3 km
0   1   2 miles

© The Guidebook Company Ltd

LAND RECLAMATION

Mention has been made in previous chapters of extensive land reclamation from the sea during the past 150 years. To give an idea of the ever-increasing scale of reclamation during the post-war period it is worth looking at where land was reclaimed in just one sample year — 1975.

From Kowloon Bay, 8.4 hectares were reclaimed for public roads and industrial development. At Kai Tak 6.8 hectares were formed for the extension of airport facilities. At Sham Shui Po 3.3 hectares were reclaimed and at the Tong Mi Road extension, 1.6 hectares. On Hong Kong Island reclamation continued with the formation of 1.7 hectares of land at Chai Wan, one hectare at Kennedy Town and 1.8 hectares in Central. In the New Territories progress was made in the reclamation of six acres at Gindrinkers Bay for industrial purposes. Also reclaimed were three acres at Shuen Wan and 0.4 hectares at the Kwai Chung incinerator site.

During the 1990s the planned development of the port and the building of Hong Kong's new airport at Chek Lap Kok, on Lantau, will provide vast areas of reclaimed land around Chek Lap Kok, off north Lantau, and around Stonecutters Island and Tsing Yi Island.

OFFICE BUILDINGS

Hong Kong Island's mighty office buildings are modern monuments to the territory's trade and prosperity. Jardine House, formerly known as the Connaught Centre, was designed by Palmer and Turner in 1973 for Jardine,Matheson and Company. The first of a new breed of skyscrapers, it was nearly double the height of its existing neighbours. The building, 52 storeys high, is studded with round windows. Since its completion others have sought to rival it.

The circular Hopewell Centre in Wan Chai was constructed at the beginning of the 1980s. Sixty-six storeys high, for a while it was the tallest building in Southeast Asia. With a revolving restaurant at the top, it glows at night like a giant cigar. The building can be entered at ground floor level from Queen's Road East, or alternatively, several floors higher from Kennedy Road. The tower was designed and built by Gordon Wu and is the corporate headquarters of Hopewell Holdings.

The towers of Exchange Square, showing the sculpture by Henry Moore in the foreground

Constructed on top of an underground station of the new Mass Transit Railway on the site of the former Naval Dockyard, Admiralty Centre was completed in 1980 and has two curtain-walled towers 27 and 33 storeys high, standing on a four-storey podium. It was designed by local architects, Wong and Ouyang.

Gloucester Tower and the atrium of the Landmark in Central were also completed in 1980, whilst the complex's second office block, Edinburgh Tower, was opened in 1983. The Landmark is famous for its prestigious shops, clustered on balconies overlooking a fountain in the atrium. It was designed by Palmer and Turner and built by the Hong Kong Land Company.

St John's Building, standing on a traffic island between Garden Road and Cotton Tree Drive, was designed by Kwan Ng Wong and Associates for the Peak Tramway Company and it was completed in 1983. The office block also houses the lower terminus of the Peak Tram. The unusual cladding on the exterior walls is cast-aluminium and the building rests on mirror-finished stainless steel columns. The site is tiny, and it is surrounded on all sides by streams of traffic.

The contrasting textures of Jardine House (left) and Exchange Square (right) in Central

Exchange Square is undoubtedly one of Hong Kong's most sophisticated and elegant office buildings. It was designed by Remo Riva and completed in 1985. Graced with sculptures by Henry Moore, Dame Elizabeth Frink and Taiwanese artist Ju Ming, Exchange Square, with its 52-storey towers of pink Spanish granite and reflective glass, houses the Hong Kong Stock Exchange, a bus terminus, shops and offices. Art exhibitions are mounted in the Rotunda. The second office tower, Exchange Square Three, was opened in 1988.

The Royal Navy erected the eye-catching Prince of Wales Building in HMS Tamar in 1980 when Victoria Barracks was handed back to the Hong Kong Government. In 1981 the old Royal Navy China Fleet Club in Wan Chai was pulled down and a commercial building, Fleet House, was built on the site. Today the China Fleet Club still occupies the same site, but it is located in the first eight floors of the shapely, curved 25-storey tower block designed by Wong Tung and Partners.

Visitors arriving by ferry from Macau are greeted by the scarlet bands of the Shun Tak Centre's twin towers. The eastern 41-storey tower is occupied by the Victoria Hotel; the western tower houses offices. The whole ferry terminal complex was designed by Spence Robinson and completed in 1986. The inner and outer piers, housing immigration, customs and waiting lounges for ferry passengers, are connected by three of the world's largest single-span pedestrian bridges.

The Bond Centre, named after the Australian entrepreneur Alan Bond, can be counted as one of Hong Kong's most controversial and interesting office blocks. Designed by American architect, Paul Rudolph, the two hexagonal towers sit on a four-storey podium. The many facets of the irregular glass walls reflect sunlight and cast shadows at all angles, providing constant variety and visual interest. It was completed in 1988.

These are but a few of the territory's many·innovative office buildings, but they are some of Hong Kong's most obvious landmarks.

BANKS

On Hong Kong Island the banks have long dominated the architecture of Central, the HongkongBank and the Bank of China competing to built the biggest and best headquarters.

The circular tower of the Hopewell Centre, Wan Chai

The old Bank of China Building standing between Queen's Road Central and Des Voeux Road, designed by the Chinese Nationalists after the Second World War, was to be 20 feet higher than the former Hongkong and Shanghai Bank building. It was completed by the Communists after they came to power, and two Chinese lions stand sentinel outside, rivalling the lions of the HongkongBank next door.

HongkongBank replaced its pre-war headquarters in the mid-1980s with a *tour de force* designed by the English architect, Norman Foster. Constructed at a cost of HK$5.3 billion, the pale grey edifice is functional, awe-inspiring and majestic, reflecting the role of the Bank in the territory.

Not to be outdone, the Bank of China commissioned the brilliant Chinese-American architect, I M Pei, to design a bigger and more impressive building. The new Bank of China Tower was completed in 1989, and it looks down on every other building in Central. It is the tallest building outside New York and Chicago. Shaped like an angular bamboo shoot, it rises as a series of triangular prisms culminating in twin masts at the summit.

Whether the building is haunted by the ghost of Murray House, which it unceremoniously displaced, or whether it is simply a source of bad *feng shui*, the local press has noted that a willow tree was carefully planted in the grounds of Government House to ward off any ephemeral evil influences from the Bank of China.

In 1989, the Standard Chartered Bank completed a new building on the site of its old headquarters in Queen's Road Central. Tall and slim, it stands a little taller than its neighbour, the HongkongBank headquarters.

The Bank of Tokyo building near Queensway is an appropriate golden colour. Standing amongst rectangular white office blocks, it has been given the soubriquet 'the Amah's Tooth'.

CULTURAL COMPLEXES

It used to be said that Hong Kong was a cultural desert. However, the activities of Hong Kong people during the past twenty years have put paid to this criticism. Not only does Hong Kong now have a thriving arts scene, probably the best in the region, it also has interesting buildings in which to stage local and international arts events.

The Hong Kong Arts Centre in North Wan Chai was completed in 1977. Its design, by Tao Ho Design Architects, is ingenious, bearing in mind the very small size of the site and the severely restricted construction budget. The recital hall, studio theatre, rehearsal room, main theatre and exhibition gallery have been stacked on top of one another and the building also contains restaurants and eight floors of offices.

The cream, egg-shaped dome of the Space Museum housing a planetarium, was built by the Urban Council in 1980 on the Kowloon waterfront and is now part of the Hong Kong Cultural Centre complex. Completed in 1989, the Cultural Centre contains a concert hall seating more than 2,000, a theatre seating 1,750, a studio theatre and a range of other facilities.

Both buildings occupy a commanding position on the edge of the harbour, leading many people to question why neither structure has been endowed with windows from which one could obtain one of the finest views in the world.

The Academy for Performing Arts, designed by Simon Kwan and Associates for the Royal Hong Kong Jockey Club, is composed of schools for drama, music, dancing and theatre technology. It is located in North Wan Chai and was opened in 1985. Planned as a cluster of triangular prisms, it contains a number of public theatres, recital halls, practice rooms, dance studios and other facilities.

The Hong Kong Coliseum, completed in 1983, was a large-scale addition to Hong Kong's cultural facilities. The white, futuristic-looking stadium is built above railway lines and goods train platforms on a podium. It seats 15,000 people and is used for sports events, conventions, exhibitions, stage performances and ice-skating shows.

Most opulent of all, Hong Kong's gleaming iridescent Convention and Exhibition Centre on the North Wan Chai waterfront incorporates exhibition centres, conference rooms, theatres and a hotel in one vast complex. Designed by Augustine Lee of Ng Chun Man, the Convention and

The Bond Centre, Central

Exhibition Centre was officially opened by the Prince and Princess of Wales in 1989.

RELIGIOUS BUILDINGS

The tranquil Ching Chung Koon (Green Pine Temple) was built in 1949 at Tuen Mun in the New Territories by Taoists, followers of the fourth century BC philosopher, Lao Zi. It is dedicated to one of the Eight Immortals, Lu Sun Young, and two of his disciples. The temple is famous for its collection of 4,000 books on Taoism and Chinese history, as well as for its collection of bonsai in the temple precincts.

At Sha Tin, the building of the Buddhist Temple of Ten Thousand Buddhas was completed in 1957 by the Abbot, Yuet Kai. In the main temple high on a hillside, there are more than 12,000 gilded images of Buddha, each with different gestures. The courtyard outside has larger than life-size statues of various Buddhist saints, whilst at the far end a nine-storey pink pagoda overlooks the Sha Tin valley.

The Reverend Yuet Kai died in 1965 at the age of 87. Eight months after his burial his body was unearthed and, as he had foretold, it had not decayed. Regarded as a miracle by his followers, Yuet Kai's body was gilded and mounted in a glass case in a shrine, where it can still be seen today.

The temple of Wong Tai Sin in north Kowloon is one of the biggest, busiest and most colourful in the territory. It was built in 1973 on the site of a previous temple to Wong Tai Sin founded in 1921. Wong Tai Sin was a shepherd who lived in Zhejiang provice in China. Legend has it that at the age of fifteen he was taught by an immortal how to produce a drug from the mineral cinnabar, to heal the sick. His help is sought by the sick, and worship at his temple is thought to be highly efficacious.

In 1981 a columbarium, designed by Ng Chun Man and Associates to accord with traditional Chinese concepts of architecture, was completed at Cape Collinson. It contains 19,600 niches which each hold two sets of ashes from cremations. Incorporating principles from the Chinese third-century classic, the *Book of Changes*, the elegant and harmonious structure is octagonal, with the windows on each face arranged in six broken rows like hexagrams.

By contrast, the Hung Hom Funeral Parlour in Kowloon

The upper reaches of the Bank of China tower, completed in 1989

157

appears ominous, displaying its dreadful warning: one side of the building is covered with a giant illuminated cigarette advertisement.

HOTELS

The American Hilton Hotel group was the first international chain to establish itself in Hong Kong in the 1960s. Situated on the corner of Garden Road, the Hilton was one of Hong Kong's earliest skyscrapers.

The Mandarin, built by the Hong Kong Land Company in 1963, is regularly voted the hotel with the best service in the world. It is probably Hong Kong's finest and most famous hotel.

In the 1970s and 1980s a plethora of new hotels was erected on both sides of the harbour, particularly in the reclaimed area of Tsim Sha Tsui East. They dazzle and sparkle in the sunshine, their windows reflecting the waters of the harbour which they overlook.

By 1990 Hong Kong hotels had become ever more elaborate. The Regent and the Marriott Hotel, like many others, constitute part of a much larger shopping complex, and the Grand Hyatt is an integral part of the new Convention and Exhibition Centre.

Older hotels have been rebuilt, most notably the Repulse Bay Hotel and the Luk Kwok in Wan Chai. The charming old Repulse Bay Hotel on the south side of the Island was pulled down in the early 1980s when the owners wished to redevelop the site. The widespread public dismay at the passing of a much-loved haunt inspired the owners to build a replica of the hotel's façade. The verandahs, housing restaurants, are located in front of a new multi-storey apartment block.

The replica, although pleasant, does not capture the essence of the original building, overshadowed as it is by the gaudy Miami-style apartment block behind. Nonetheless, the episode demonstrated the strength of feeling harboured by Hong Kong people about one of their favourite places.

Few felt sentimental about the passing of the old Luk Kwok Hotel on which Richard Mason based his description of the Nam Kwok waterfront bordello in *The World of Suzie Wong*. Today the new Luk Kwok in Gloucester Road is a restrained, attractive building with Art Deco influences.

The Wong Tai Sin temple in North Kowloon

CLUBS

The redevelopment of the old Hong Kong Club overlooking Statue Square, caused much bitterness amongst conservationists in the territory. Despite a petition to the Queen, the gracious colonnaded building was demolished in 1981 to make way for more economic and efficient high-rise premises.

The new Hong Kong Club building which has risen in its place was designed by the Australian, Harry Seidler, and completed in 1985. It is smart and comfortable, and provides impressive facilities for the Club, but many still mourn the loss of the old building which formed part of the heart of Hong Kong.

In contrast, the Royal Hong Kong Jockey Club Members' Clubhouse at the Sha Tin racecourse is bright and cheerful. The balconies rising in tiers, painted light grey with pillar-box red metalwork and trailing plants, reflect the jolly spirit of racegoers. It was designed by Prescott and Partners and completed in 1985.

The Convention and Exhibition Centre, Wan Chai

UNIVERSITIES AND POLYTECHNICS

Situated on a steep slope, Robert Black College at the University of Hong Kong was built in two phases, the first phase in 1965 and the second in 1973. Although the architects, Szeto Wai and Partners, used modern materials they incorporated traditional Chinese domestic design concepts, such as blue roof tiles, balconies and courtyards, to produce peaceful and harmonious accommodation for visiting scholars.

Szeto Wai and Partners also designed the campus of the new Chinese University at Sha Tin in 1964. Much of the construction was completed in the early 1970s. Standing on a hill overlooking Tolo Harbour, the stark, minimalist, concrete buildings of the campus are reminiscent of the new universities of the 1960s in Britain and America.

The red-brick campus of the Hong Kong Polytechnic in Kowloon was designed by Palmer and Turner in 1973. Construction was completed by the beginning of the 1980s. With only a very small site to accommodate a major tertiary institution, the architects designed the campus in flexible modules. The classrooms and lecture rooms are stacked on top of a podium overlooking an inner courtyard. Services are contained in the cylindrical cores linking the classroom blocks.

TEN TOURS TO HISTORIC PLACES IN HONG KONG

The following itineraries provide some ideas for planning expeditions to historic places in Hong Kong. If you are not familiar with the urban areas or the New Territories, you may find it difficult to get to some of the places, and you may also find it it difficult to judge how long to allow for the journey.

Don't be put off! These itineraries give some suggestions about what you can do comfortably in a day. Time schedules have been included as a guide, and with the opening hours of some places in mind, but you may prefer to set your own pace.

While some of the historic sites are not open to visitors or are difficult to reach, they are worth a visit from an architectural or archaeological standpoint.

It is worth bearing in mind that during the summer, less energetic people will find some expeditions too long and tiring in the heat, whereas in the winter others might try to include more places.

Once you are familiar with the transport system, you will probably want to get right off the beaten track and explore the territory's less accessible historic sites. Whatever you decide to do, have fun! There is usually something of historic interest wherever you go in Hong Kong.

1. CENTRAL AND THE PEAK *(map 1)*

0900 Walk from the Star Ferry Hong Kong to Jardine House (1). Cross Connaught Road Central on the overhead walkway, turn left and walk past the Mandarin Hotel (2) to Statue Square (10 minutes).

0915 The Hong Kong Club (3), located between Connaught Road Central and Chater Road, overlooks the Cenotaph next to Statue Square. On the opposite side of Chater Road stands the Legislative Council (4) (the Old Supreme Court).

0930 Walk south of Statue Square and reach the HongkongBank Building (5). Take a trip up the escalator to the upper level. To the west of the Bank is the Standard Chartered Bank (6). South of both banks, in Queen's Road Central, is the Hilton Hotel (7). East of the Hilton is the huge Bank of China Tower (8), resembling an angular bamboo shoot.

0950 Walk up Garden Road behind the Hilton (10 minutes) to the Peak Tram Station (9) (St John's Building). Do not take the Peak Tram yet, but turn left, and follow the sign to the Urban Council Squash Centre on Cotton Tree Drive (3 minutes). A little further down from the Squash Centre is the road leading to the Flagstaff House Museum of Tea Ware (10) (3 minutes).

1010 Spend 30 minutes at the Flagstaff House Museum of Tea Ware. (Open daily, except Wednesdays and some public holidays, 10 am–5 pm.)

1040 Return to the Peak Tram Station. Take the Peak Tram to the Peak (12 minutes).

1100 Stroll along Lugard Road and Harlech Road and enjoy the panoramic views to north and south over the harbour and the outlying islands (1 hour).

1215 Lunch at the Peak Café opposite the upper terminus.

1315 Return by tram to Central. Walk down the left side of Garden Road and enter St. John's Cathedral (11) through the wrought iron gate (Battery Path) (3 minutes). The French Mission Building (12) stands beside the Cathedral on the north side, just behind the Hilton Hotel.

1345 From the French Mission Building walk down Battery Path (13) and continue westwards along Queen's Road Central, turning left into Duddell Street after the Sing Pao Centre. Duddell Street steps and gas lamps (14) are at the end of the cul-de-sac (6 minutes).

1410 Continue along Queen's Road Central westwards, turning left into D'Aguilar Street and then right into Stanley Street. The Luk Yu Teahouse and Restaurant (15) is located at No 26 (6 minutes).

1425   Walk further up Stanley Street and left into Pottinger Street. Climb the steps until you reach Hollywood Road. Immediately opposite is Central Police Station with the Magistracy and Jail behind (16) (5 minutes). From Central Police Station walk down Hollywood Road and turn into Wyndham Street (6 minutes). The Foreign Correspondents' Club, which now occupies part of the Old Dairy Farm Building (17), is located between Wyndham Street and Lower Albert Road. The Bishop's House (18) is opposite the Old Dairy Farm Building, standing high above the traffic.

1500   Continue down Wyndham Street to Queen's Road Central and cross the road into Pedder Street (5 minutes). Pedder Building (19) is on the left and the Landmark shopping centre is on the right. Notice the red oval plaque between 3A Pedder Street and the Landmark (20), just above eye level, which marks the waterfront of Hong Kong as it was in 1841.

Continue down Pedder Street, crossing the road at the traffic lights. There is another red oval plaque at the corner of Swire House (Pedder Street and Chater Road) which marks the waterfront of Hong Kong between 1843 and 1865. Take the overhead walkway across Connaught Road Central, passing Exchange Square (21) on your left (5 minutes). Then take the stairs down to ground level, next to Jardine House.

1520   Cross to the Star Ferry concourse then on to the City Hall High Block which houses the Museum of Art (22) on the tenth and eleventh floors (4 minutes). It is open 10 am–6 pm daily, except Thursdays and some public holidays.

1600   Return to the Star Ferry, Hong Kong (2 minutes).

2. MID-LEVELS AND WESTERN *(map 1)*

0930   Walk from the Star Ferry Hong Kong to Connaught Road Central behind Jardine House (3 minutes). Take bus No 3 or bus No 12 to Caine Road (10 minutes). Alight at the Caritas Centre after sighting Government House on the right.

164

0945 On the left is the entrance to the Hong Kong Zoological & Botanical Gardens(23), and on the right, behind the Caritas Centre is the Roman Catholic Cathedral (24). Visit both the garden (30 minutes) and the cathedral (15 minutes).

1045 Continue along Caine Road to the new Sacred Heart Canossian Convent College. Behind it is the Sacred Heart Canossian Convent Chapel (25).

1115 Turn left and go up Shelley Street to reach Jamia Mosque (26) behind the old yellow building (Leong Fee Terrace). Visitors may enter the mosque to look around.

1130 Continue up Shelley Street and walk up the steps until you reach Robinson Road. Turn right and walk westwards (15 minutes).

1145 Beyond the Seymour Road turning and Castle Steps you will find the Ohel Leah Synagogue (27) on the right, tucked into the hillside below the road. (The Synagogue is now under renovation. Opening hours after renovation are not yet available.)

1200 Turn right off Robinson Road and walk down along Castle Road (10 minutes). You will see a red brick house on the right. It was originally a residence and is at present used as the Church of Jesus Christ of Latter-Day Saints. Cross the road and walk to the left (10 minutes) till you see Ladder Street on the right. Walk down Ladder Street (3 minutes) and find Man Mo Temple (28) on Hollywood Road. Alternatively, you may wish to take a taxi to Man Mo Temple (5 minutes' ride). Spend 20 minutes at the temple.

1245 Walk westwards along Hollywood Road (5 minutes), turn left into Upper Station Street and reach Tai Ping Shan Street. Turn right, and Kwong Fuk Tse Temple and Ancestral Hall (29) is at the corner of Pound Lane and Tai Ping Shan Street.

1300 Return to Hollywood Road, and Possession Street(30) is just to the left on the opposite side of Hollywood Road.

1315 Lunch at one of the restaurants in the area.

1430 At the other end of Possession Street is Queen's Road Central. Cross the road and walk east along Queen's Road Central till you reach Morrison Street on the left (3 minutes). Walk to the end of Morrison Street until you reach Connaught Road Central where you will see the tramway. The distinctive Western Market (31) is on your left, facing Connaught Road Central. Note the exterior of the Market; the building is under renovation and not yet open to visitors.

1500 Turn eastwards along Connaught Road Central, and you will see the Shun Tak Centre and the Macau Ferry Terminal on your left. Go up to the second floor of the Shun Tak Centre and take the walkway above the ground back to the Star Ferry (20 minutes).

3. SOUTH HONG KONG ISLAND *(map 2)*

0900 Walk from the Star Ferry Hong Kong to Connaught Road Central behind Jardine House (3 minutes). Take bus No 3 (about 15 minutes). Get off at the stop in front of the University of Hong Kong, opposite St Paul's Boys' College on Bonham Road.

0920 Just before the University main entrance is the Fung Ping Shan Museum (1). Spend about 20 minutes in the Museum. (Open 9.30 am–6.00 pm except Sundays and some public holidays.)

0945 Enter the University campus up a sharp ramp. Walk past the Main Building (2) (or Loke Yew Hall) and the old Senior Common Room (3) opposite. Walk straight ahead and exit through the western gate.

1000 Take No 7 bus from the stop in front of Haking Wong Building on Pokfulam Road.

1015 Alight opposite Woodbury Court (two stops after Queen Mary Hospital) and turn left up the road leading to the University residences (142 Pokfulam Road), and

University Hall (Douglas Castle) (4) is on the left. Permission is required for entrance to University Hall; the exterior is worth noting. Follow the path past the building down to Pokfulam Reservoir Road. Walk down past Pokfulam Riding School and then cross Pokfulam Road.

1035 Go up the drive leading to Hong Kong University Press (Bethanie) (5) at 139 Pokfulam Road. If you wish to see round the building, an appointment should be made beforehand with the Publisher (telephone 550 2703).

Continue along Pokfulam Road for one minute until you reach Pokfulam Temporary Housing Area on your right. Walk through the housing area until the black roofs of the octagonal Old Dairy Farm Cowsheds (6) are visible.

Retrace your steps to the main road.

1055 Take a taxi to Nam Fung Road in Wong Chuk Hang (about 10 minutes). Notice Wah Fu Estate on the right before you reach Aberdeen.

1115 Get off at Wong Chuk Hang Pumping Substation opposite Nam Fung Temporary Housing Area on Nam Fung Road. Just before the substation find the sign for the Ancient Rock Carving. Follow the sign and climb the steep path for one minute to reach the Ancient Rock Carving(7).

Walk back to Nam Fung Road and cross the road. Turn right and walk down to Wong Chuk Hang Road (3 minutes). Take the overhead pass on the left to the traffic island. Cross the road to the right and keep walking (2 minutes). Find the bus stop before Shouson Hill Road. Take either No 73 bus or No 260 to Stanley. Get off at the bus terminus opposite Stanley Road playground.

1235 Lunch in one of Stanley's Chinese or European restaurants.

1330 Walk along Stanley Market Road to the Tin Hau Temple (8) (5 minutes). It is beyond Stanley Beach down the lane leading through Ma Hang village. Spend 15 minutes at the temple. As you walk along the beachfront notice the military buildings of Stanley Fort at the end of the Stanley Peninsula. This is a closed area and visitors may not enter without permission.

From the temple return by the same route to Stanley Village Road and turn right. The Southern District Office (the Old Police Station) (9) stands beside the Wellcome supermarket.

1400 From the Southern District Office continue walking along Stanley Village Road, turning into Wong Ma Kok Road and passing St Stephen's College playing fields on the left and a path to St Stephen's Beach on the right.

1420 Stanley Military Cemetery (10) is on the left of the road, marked by a small car park and a flight of steps. Walk up the steps to the cemetery.

Walk back to Stanley Bus Terminus (20 minutes) and then take bus No 6 or No 260 back to Exchange Square Bus Terminus in Central (40 minutes).

4. KOWLOON–TSIM SHA TSUI *(map 3)*

0900 Walk from Kowloon Star Ferry towards the right (1 minute). The Old Kowloon–Canton Railway Station Clocktower (1) is clearly visible from the Pier.

Notice the Marine Police Headquarters (2) opposite the Cultural Centre on the north side of Salisbury Road.

0910 Walk behind the Clocktower and enter the Hong Kong Cultural Centre (3).

0920 Walk eastwards along Salisbury Road and cross the road to the Peninsula Hotel (4).

0930 Walk towards Signal Hill Garden (5) (10 minutes). First cross Nathan Road to the Sheraton Hotel. Head for Middle Road behind the Sheraton. Just before the Mariner's Club on Middle Road find the alley on the left leading to Minden Row. The entrance to Signal Hill Garden is located on your right hand side. The Garden is open daily from 7 am to 11 pm. Walk up the hill (3 minutes) to the Signal Tower. The tower is open daily (9 am–11 am and 4 pm–6 pm).

1015 Leave the garden and continue up Minden Row to Mody Road. Turn left into Mody Road and then right at the Holiday Inn into Nathan Road. Walk northwards for two blocks and cross Nathan Road. Reach the MTR Station beside the shining domes of the modern Kowloon Mosque (Jamia Masjid) (6). The mosque is not open to visitors without an appointment.

1030 Enter Kowloon Park via the entrance next to the mosque on Nathan Road. Bear right, walking uphill (5 minutes) until you reach the Hong Kong Museum of History (7) in the middle of the park.

1115 Leave the park and return to Nathan Road. Cross Nathan Road and walk northwards (3 minutes) until you reach the Tsim Sha Tsui District Kai Fong Welfare Association (Old Kowloon British School) (8). An uphill road here leads you to the Royal Observatory. (Visitors cannot enter without prior permission.)

A little further on, along Nathan Road, is St Andrew's Church (9).

1130 Continue walking up Nathan Road (20 minutes or 800 metres) until you reach the Chinese Temple (Tin Hau Temple) (10) on Public Square Street, left of Nathan Road. Alternatively, you may take bus No 2, 6, 6A or 7 going northwards. Get off the bus after spotting the flyover across Nathan Road. Public Square Street is two streets after the flyover.

1230 Lunch in one of Kowloon's many Chinese and international restaurants.

Afternoon (optional): for those visitors who would like to visit Boundary Street.

1400 Take bus No 7 from in front of the King's Hotel on Nathan Road (10 minutes). Get off at the Kowloon Tong Club on Waterloo Road. While crossing the flyover, notice St Teresa's Parish Church on the left of the flyover. Walk back until you reach Boundary Street (3 minutes).

1420 Cross Waterloo Road, and the red-bricked Maryknoll Convent School is in front of you.

Walk northwards up Waterloo Road (3 minutes). Just after Flint Road, there is a bus stop. Take bus No 7 back to the Star Ferry Kowloon.

5. NORTH KOWLOON AND TSUEN WAN *(map 4)*

0900   Take bus No 5 from the Kowloon Star Ferry bus terminus.

0920   Alight outside Argyle Street Sports Ground. Hong Kong International Airport can be seen on the right. Walk back along the road (3 minutes) and cross Ma Tau Chung Road to reach the entrance of Sung Wong Toi Park (1) where the Sung Wong Toi terrace is located.

0940   Leave the park and walk along the main road towards the airport (10 minutes). Cross Prince Edward Road East by the pedestrian subway and walk towards the Regal Airport Hotel. Turn left into Sa Po Road, beside the hotel, and continue walking until you reach Tung Tsing Road. Walk up Tung Tsing Road (3 minutes) and Kowloon Walled City (2) is on the left, identified by the many dentists' shops. Look at the outside, but do not venture in as it is very easy to get lost.

1040   Depart from the Walled City by Tung Tau Tsuen Road. Visit the Hau Wong Temple (3) on the right at the end of Tung Tau Tsuen Road. The Crane and Goose Inscription is beside the temple.

1100   Walk up Junction Road (10 minutes) to Lok Fu MTR Station near the junction of Junction Road and Wang Tau Hom East Road. Take the MTR to Wong Tai Sin, the next station. There is a directional sign showing how to get to Wong Tai Sin Temple from the MTR station.

1130   Visit Wong Tai Sin Temple (4).

1200   Lunch at one of the restaurants in the area.

1315   Take the MTR from Wong Tai Sin to Prince Edward MTR Station. Cross the platform and change from the MTR Tsuen Wan line to reach Cheung Sha Wan. Leave the MTR Station by the Tonkin Street exit, turn left and walk to the Han tomb, Lei Cheng Uk (5). Return to Cheung Sha Wan MTR Station. Examples of the first public housing estates can be seen on the right. Take the MTR to Tsuen Wan.

1415   From Tsuen Wan MTR Station, follow the signs for Sam Tung Uk Museum (6) (10 minutes).

1500   Departing from the Museum, take the overhead walkway to the other side of Castle Peak Road and walk along Chung On Street (3 minutes), turning left into Tsuen Wan Market Street. Hoi Pa Village House (7) is inside a small garden. (A use for the house is being considered, so visitors can only appreciate the exterior for the time being.)

1545   Return to Tsuen Wan MTR Station and take the MTR to Tsim Sha Tsui Station.

6. LANTAU—TUNG CHUNG *(map 5)*

0815   Take the ferry from the Outlying Districts Services Pier, west of the Central Star Ferry, to Silvermine Bay (Mui Wo 梅窩), Lantau.

0925   Arrive on Lantau. Take bus No 3 (departs at 0935) from Silvermine Bay to Tung Chung, from the bus terminal in front of the ferry pier. (The next bus departs at 1150.)

1015   Arrive at Tung Chung and walk to Hau Wong Temple (1) by the sea (30 minutes).

1100   Return to Tung Chung Road and visit Tung Chung Fort (2) .

1200   Leave Tung Chung Fort and walk to Tung Chung village at the end of the road, passing Tung Chung Battery (3) on the way (10 minutes).

1245   Lunch at one of the restaurants in Tung Chung village.

1335   Return to Silvermine Bay by bus No 3 from the terminus in Tung Chung Village.

1420   On arrival at Silvermine Bay, visit the Li Family Taxation Stone (4) in the garden opposite the ferry pier.

1425   Return to Hong Kong Island by ferry.

1600   Arrive at the Outlying Districts Services Pier in Central.

7. LANTAU–PO LIN AND TAI O *(map 5)*

0815   Depart from the Outlying Districts Services Pier, west of the Central Star Ferry, to Silvermine Bay (Mui Wo 梅窩), Lantau.

0925   Arrive at Silvermine Bay and take bus No 1 (heading for Tai O 大澳) to Shek Pik.

1000   Get off at the bus stop opposite Shek Pik Reservoir. Walk downhill to the left, until you reach the Rock Carving (5) (20 minutes). The archaeological site at Shek Pik is on the beach. (There is no sign for it.)

1100   Walk back to the main road (15 minutes) and take bus No 2 heading to Ngong Ping (昂坪) to Po Lin Monastery (6))(寶蓮寺¹) (15 minutes).

1145   Arrive at Po Lin Monastery, and buy a lunch ticket from the Monastery office before you explore the grounds.

1230   Enjoy a vegetarian lunch in the Monastery's dining hall.

1345   Depart from Po Lin Monastery by bus No 2 heading for Mui Wo.

1355   Alight at the junction of Keung Shau Road (羌山道) and Sham Wat Road (深屈道), and change to bus No 1 to Tai O.

1430   On arrival at the Tai O bus terminus and before walking into the village (past Tai O Police Reporting Centre) check the District Board Map for directions to Market Street. Cross the creek by rope-drawn sampan. Turn right and walk to the end of Market Street and across the causeway to Hau Wong Temple (7) (20 minutes). Retrace your steps

172

to the bus terminus at Tai O. (Tai O Police Station is at Shek Tsui Po, the other end of Tai O Island. It takes about 30 minutes to walk to the Police Station from Hau Wong Temple.)

1545   Return to Silvermine Bay (Mui Wo) by bus No 1.

1645   Return to Hong Kong Island by ferry.

1800   Arrive in Central at the Outlying Districts Services Pier.

8. TUEN MUN, PING SHAN AND KAM TIN *(map 6)*
   This itinerary is for adventurous visitors only.

Most of the villagers and taxi/bus drivers do not speak English. You may wish to hire a car to go to these places, but be sure you advise the driver beforehand of the places you wish to visit. Alternatively, you may wish to hire a freelance guide through the HARTCO (Hong Kong Association of Registered Tour-Coordinators) Membership Directory, to accompany you on the journey (especially if you wish to continue the trip after Tsui Shing Lau). Telephone: 802 6063.

0900   Take the hoverferry from Blake Pier, west of the Star Ferry in Central, to Tuen Mun (35 minutes).

0950   Take Light Rail Transit (LRT) No 506, 610 or 611 from Tuen Mun ferry pier to Butterfly Station (approximately 8 minutes). As you approach the station there is a temporary housing site on the left. Walk back towards it and go through a red arch inscribed with Chinese characters. Continue until you reach Hung Lau (1), a two-storey red house (10 minutes).

   Spend 10 minutes at Hung Lau.

1030   Return to Butterfly Station and take the LRT to Technical Institute Station (10 minutes). Walk up the hill, passing between the Technical Institute and St Peter's Church, until you reach Castle Peak Monastery (2)(青山寺) (40 minutes' walk). Less energetic visitors may wish to take a taxi. Ask the taxi driver to take you right up the hill to the entrance of Castle Peak Monastery. It is a long walk up, if you alight at the bottom.

Spend 20 minutes there.

1145   Return to Technical Institute Station and take LRT No 610 to Shek Pai Station. Change to LRT No 505 for Ching Chung Station (35 minutes).

1215   Arrive at Ching Chung Koon Taoist Temple (3). Explore the grounds and enjoy a vegetarian lunch. Buy a lunch coupon from the temple office. (No advance reservation is needed.)

1400   Take LRT No 505 from Ching Chung Koon Station to Siu Hong Station. Change here and take any train for Yuen Long. Alight at Ping Shan Station. (15 minutes.)

1415   Exit from Ping Shan Station and walk straight ahead. Turn left into Ping Ha Road (屏廈路).

1425   When you see the sign post for Tong Fong Tsuen (塘坊村), turn right towards the village on the opposite side of the street.

1430   Kun Ting Study Hall (4) (覲廷書室) is on your right as you approach the village.

1500   Turn right as you leave the study hall and walk straight ahead. After two minutes' walk, you will find the Tang Ancestral Hall (鄧氏宗祠) on your right. (It is now under renovation, and it has not yet been decided whether it will be opened to the public.)

1515   Exit the Ancestral Hall, go staight along the path to the right and you will see the Hang Tau Tsuen (坑頭村) sign post. Take the first left turn after passing a few small shops.

1525   After passing a farm on your left and rows of one-storey houses, you will find a fish pond on your right.

174

1545   Tsui Shing Lau Pagoda (5) (聚星樓) is opposite the fish pond.

1605   Walk back to the main road (Ping Ha Road) (屏夏路). Take feeder bus No 655 heading for Yuen Long East (元朗東).

1615   When you see the blue road sign for Kik Yeung Road (擊壤路) on your left, press the bell and get off at Yuen Long Plaza. You will alight at Castle Peak Road opposite the Fung Nin Road (豐年路) LRT Station.

Walk east along Castle Peak Road and turn left when you see Kik Yeung Road, the bus terminus.

EITHER:

Take bus No 68M heading for Tsuen Wan MTR station (50 minutes). Catch the MTR back to Central (30 minutes).

OR:

Energetic and adventurous visitors may continue the following itinerary.
    Take bus No 54 heading for Sheung Tsuen (上村) to continue your journey to Kam Tin.

1645   After the bus has passed the Shek Kong (石崗) signpost, look for a white signboard on your left for 水頭村 /水尾村 only in Chinese. Press the bell when you see the white board. Kam Tin Walled Village (6) (吉慶圍) is just opposite the bus stop. The entrance fee is HK$1 per person.

1715   Take bus No 51 heading for Tsuen Wan Ferry Pier. The bus stop is on the same side of the street as Kam Tin Walled Village (40 minutes).

1755   Get off at the bus terminus and take the hoverferry back to Central.

9. SHEUNG SHUI *(map 7)*

0850   Board bus No 8 or 5C from Star Ferry Bus Terminal, Kowloon to Kowloon Railway Station, Hung Hom (10 minutes).

0900 Depart by Kowloon–Canton Railway (KCR) train to Sheung Shui.

0940 Arrive at Sheung Shui Station. Take bus No 76K heading for Yuen Long (元朗) from the Shek Wu Hui (石湖墟) bus terminal opposite Sheung Shui Station or take red minibus No 17 (元朗) from San Fat Street (新發街) opposite the station. When you see the blue road sign for San Tin (新田) on your left, press the bell and get off the bus. (If you take a minibus, show the Chinese name (我想去新田，請指示落車) to the driver when getting on the minibus.)

1020 Arrive at San Tin Village. Follow the sign (大夫第) (in Chinese only) and walk for five minutes to Tai Fu Tai (1).

1030 Visit Tai Fu Tai. (Open 9 am–1 pm and 2 pm–5 pm daily, except Tuesdays, Christmas Day, Boxing Day, New Year's Day and the first three days of Chinese New Year. Admission is free.)

1050 Leave Tai Fu Tai; walk through San Tin Village and walk for five minutes to Man Lun Fung Ancestral Hall (no sign on the way) (文公麟峯祠).

1055 Visit Man Lun Fung Ancestral Hall (2).

1115 Return to the entrance of San Tin Village; depart for Lok Ma Chau by red minibus No 17 (上水). (Show the Chinese name (我想去落馬洲，請指示落車) to the driver when getting on the bus.) Alight at the junction of Castle Peak Road and Lok Ma Chau Road; then walk for 20 minutes along Lok Ma Chau Road to the lookout.

1140 Visit Lok Ma Chau lookout (3).

1200 Return to the beginning of Lok Ma Chau Road; take bus No 76K, or red minibus No 17 (上水) to Sheung Shui Station.

1215 Arrive at Sheung Shui Station and have lunch in Sheung Shui Town.

176

1315 Walk back to Sheung Shui Station. Change to green minibus No 55K (沙頭角) from the green minibus terminal next to the Railway Station for San Wai (10 minutes). (Show the Chinese note saying 我想去宣道園，請指示落車 to the driver of the minibus when getting on.)

1325 Alight at Suen Douh Camp (宣道園) at San Wai Village. Walk along the lane as indicated by the road sign Kun Lung Gate (觀龍圍) for ten minutes to Kun Lung Gate Tower.

1335 Visit Kun Lung Gate Tower (4).

1350 Return to the entrance of San Wai Village. Catch green minibus No 55K (上水) for Sheung Shui Station (10 minutes).

1400 Arrive at Sheung Shui Station. Catch the train for Hung Hom (35 minutes).

1435 Arrive at Kowloon Railway Station. Board bus No 8 or 5C for Star Ferry Bus Terminal, Kowloon.

10. SHA TIN *(map 8)* AND TAI PO *(map 9)*

This tour is for the adventurous and energetic visitor only. It is also important to watch your time: the Railway Museum at Tai Po closes at 4 pm.

0830 From the MTR station in Tsim Sha Tsui, take the train to Kowloon Tong (25 minutes). At Kowloon Tong MTR Station, follow the sign for Citybus and take bus No 82M to Jat Min Chuen, Sha Tin (the first stop after the Lion Rock Tunnel) (30 minutes).

0930 Walk back down the road and cross Sha Kok Road. Turn left and continue until you reach Tsang Tai Uk Walled Village (1). Spend about 15 minutes in the village.

1000 From Tsang Tai Uk walk to Tai Chung Kiu Road and cross the bridge over the Shing Mun River (10 minutes). Turn left, enter the subway and continue straight ahead.

Turn right at the subway exit and walk under the flyover (5 minutes) and then up to Tao Fong Shan Road to the Tao Fong Shan Christian Centre (40 minutes). Most visitors may want to take a taxi up the steep hill.

Spend about 20 minutes in the Christian Centre (2).

1115   From Tao Fong Shan take the path to Pai Tau. The path is marked by a sign for Cheung Shek Kee (張石記) Stone Factory (15 minutes).

At Pai Tau, turn left and walk up the hill to the Ten Thousand Buddhas Monastery (3). Spend 20 minutes at the monastery.

1205   From the monastery, take the footpath down to Shatin KCR station (20 minutes).

1225   Take bus No 72 or 72B from the bus stop beneath New Town Plaza. As you pass the Shatin Racecourse, note the Royal Hong Kong Jockey Club Members' Clubhouse.

1305   Alight at the sign for the Yucca de Lac Restaurant in Tai Po Road.

1315   Lunch at the Yucca de Lac Restaurant, which has a terrace overlooking Tolo Harbour and the surrounding hills.

1400   Walk across Tai Po Road and you will see the front entrance to the Chinese University of Hong Kong. Go through the campus and take the shuttle bus from outside University Station (next to the stadium). Alight at the bus stop outside the Chinese University Library. The Chinese University Art Gallery is right next to the Library Building. (Open 10 am–4.30 pm daily, except Sundays and public holidays.) Spend about 30 minutes visiting the Art Gallery.

1445   Take the shuttle bus from outside the Administration Building back to the University KCR Station. Then take the train to Tai Po Market KCR Station (20 minutes). The shuttle bus runs every 20–30 minutes on a circular route through the campus.

1505   At Tai Po Market Station take the right exit and walk
for 15 minutes to the temporary market in On Fu Road.
Visit the Hong Kong Railway Museum (4). (Open 9 am–
4 pm daily, except Tuesdays.)

1620   Return to Tai Po Market Station. Take the train back
to Kowloon Tong Station (25 minutes) and change to the
MTR to return to Central. A transfer at Mongkok Station is
necessary (30 minutes).

Map 1

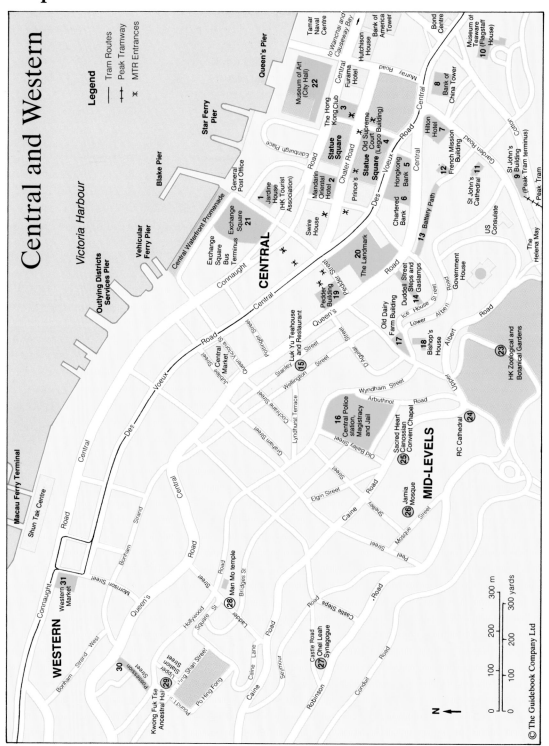

Central and Western

Victoria Harbour

Outlying Districts Services Pier

Vehicular Ferry Pier

Central Waterfront Promenade

Blake Pier

Star Ferry Pier

Queen's Pier

Tamar Naval Centre

To Wanchai and Causeway Bay

Bank of America Tower

Hutchison House

Bond Centre

Museum of Teaware 10 (Flagstaff House)

Central Furama Hotel

Museum of Art (City Hall) 22

The Hong Kong Club 3

Statue Square

Statue Square

Old Supreme Court 4 (Legco Building)

Bank of China Tower 8

Hilton Hotel 7

Hongkong Bank 5

Chartered Bank 6

French Mission Building 12

St John's Cathedral 11

St John's 9 Building

(Peak Tram terminus)

Peak Tram

Legend
— Tram Routes
‡ Peak Tramway
* MTR Entrances

Jardine House 1 (HK Tourist Association)

Mandarin Oriental Hotel 2

Swire House

General Post Office

Exchange Square 21

Exchange Square Bus Terminus

Connaught

CENTRAL

Central

Des Voeux Road

Central Road

Battery Path 13

US Consulate

The Helena May

Murray Road

Garden Road

Road

Government House

Pedder Building 19

The Landmark 20

Old Dairy Farm Building 17

Duddell Street Steps and Gaslamps 14

Bishop's House 18

Ice House Street

Lower Albert Road

Albert Road

Upper Albert Road

HK Zoological and Botanical Gardens 23

Stanley Luk Yu Teahouse and Restaurant 15

Central Market

Queen's Road

D'Aguilar Street

Stanley Street

Wellington Street

Wyndham Street

Arbuthnot Road

Central Police station, Magistracy and Jail 16

Sacred Heart Canossian Convent Chapel 25

RC Cathedral 24

MID-LEVELS

Jamia Mosque 26

Cochrane Street

Lyndhurst Terrace

Graham Street

Old Bailey Street

Caine Road

Elgin Street

Mosque Street

Shelley Street

Peel Street

Macau Ferry Terminal

Shun Tak Centre

WESTERN

Western Market 31

Connaught Road

Queen's Road

Des Voeux Road

Bonham Strand

Bonham Strand West

Morrison Street

Man Mo temple 28

Bridges St

Hollywood Road

Ladder Street

Square St

Upper Station Street

Shing Wong Street

Po Hing Fong

Castle Road

Castle Steps

Ohel Leah Synagogue 27

Kwong Fuk Tse Ancestral Hall 29

Possession Street

30

Caine Lane

Seymour Road

Robinson Road

Conduit Road

N

0   100   200   300 m
0   100   200   300 yards

© The Guidebook Company Ltd

Map 2

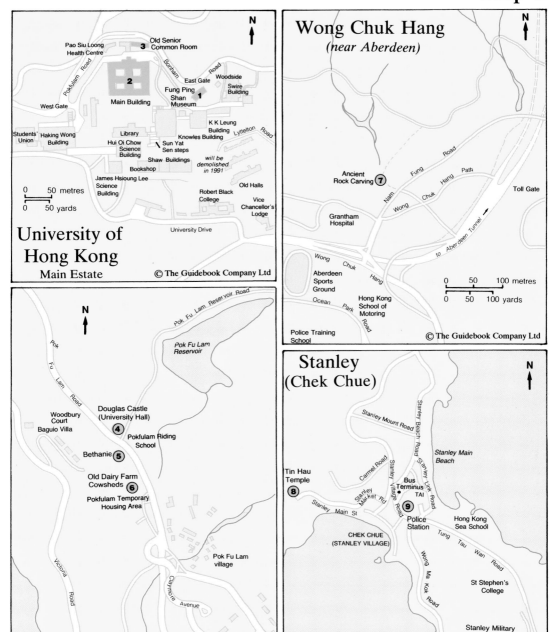

Wong Chuk Hang
(near Aberdeen)

Ancient Rock Carving (7)

Grantham Hospital

Fung Chuk Hang Road Path

Nam Wong Chuk Hang

Toll Gate

to Aberdeen Tunnel

Wong Chuk Hang

Aberdeen Sports Ground

Ocean Park Road

Hong Kong School of Motoring

Police Training School

0   50   100 metres
0   50   100 yards

© The Guidebook Company Ltd

University of Hong Kong
Main Estate

Pao Siu Loong Health Centre

3   Old Senior Common Room

Pokfulam Road

Bonham Road

2

East Gate

Woodside

Fung Ping Shan Museum   1

Swire Building

Main Building

West Gate

Students' Union

Haking Wong Building

Library

Hui Oi Chow Science Building

Knowles Building

K K Leung Building

Lyttelton Road

Sun Yat Sen steps

Shaw Buildings

will be demolished in 1991

Bookshop

James Hsioung Lee Science Building

Robert Black College

Old Halls

Vice Chancellor's Lodge

University Drive

0   50 metres
0   50 yards

© The Guidebook Company Ltd

Pokfulam

Pok Fu Lam Reservoir Road

Pok Fu Lam Reservoir

Pok Fu Lam Road

Woodbury Court

Baguio Villa

Douglas Castle (University Hall)   4

Pokfulam Riding School

Bethanie   5

Old Dairy Farm Cowsheds   6

Pokfulam Temporary Housing Area

Victoria Road

Pok Fu Lam village

Claymore Avenue

Pok Fu Lam Road

Chi Fu Fa Yuen

0   50 metres
0   50 yards

© The Guidebook Company Ltd

Stanley
(Chek Chue)

Stanley Mount Road

Stanley Beach Road

Stanley Link Road

Stanley Village Road

Stanley Main Beach

Carmel Road

Tin Hau Temple   8

Bus Terminus   TAI

Stanley Market Rd

9   Police Station

Hong Kong Sea School

Stanley Main St

CHEK CHUE (STANLEY VILLAGE)

Tung Tau Wan Road

Wong Ma Kok Road

St Stephen's College

Chek Chue Wan

Stanley Military Cemetery

10

St Stephen's Beach

Stanley Prison

To Stanley Fort

0   100   200 metres
0   100   200 yards

© The Guidebook Company Ltd

Map 3

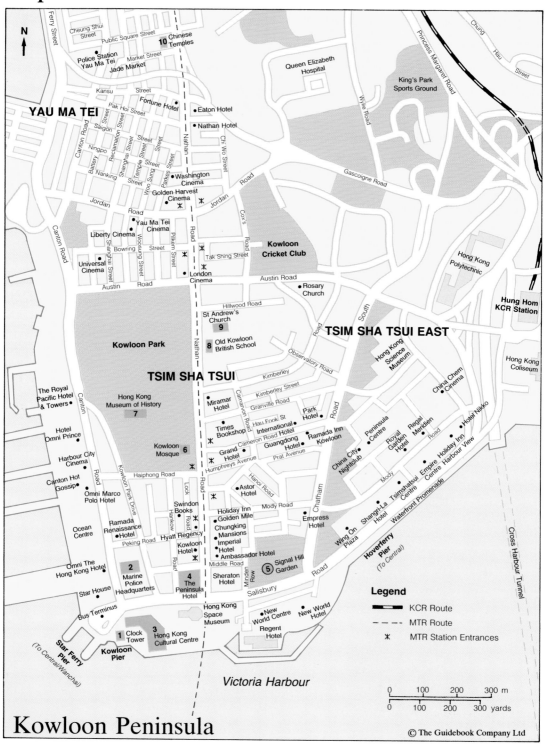

N

Ferry Street

Cheung Shui Street

Public Square Street

Market Street

10 Chinese Temples

Police Station Yau Ma Tei

Jade Market

Kansu Street

Pak Hoi Street

Saigon Street

Ningpo Street

Battery Street

Nanking Street

Canton Road

Reclamation Street

Shanghai Street

Temple Street

Woo Sung Street

Portland Street

YAU MA TEI

Fortune Hotel

Eaton Hotel

Nathan Hotel

Chi Wo Street

Nathan Road

Jordan Road

Washington Cinema

Golden Harvest Cinema

Yau Ma Tei Cinema

Liberty Cinema

Universal Cinema

Bowring Street

Woosung Street

Pilkem Street

Canton Road

Shanghai Street

Austin Road

London Cinema

Tak Shing Street

Jordan Road

Cox's Road

Kowloon Cricket Club

Queen Elizabeth Hospital

King's Park Sports Ground

Princess Margaret Road

Chung Hau Street

Wylie Road

Gascoigne Road

Hong Kong Polytechnic

Hung Hom KCR Station

Hillwood Road

Rosary Church

St Andrew's Church

9

8 Old Kowloon British School

TSIM SHA TSUI EAST

South Road

Observatory Road

Hong Kong Science Museum

China Chem Cinema

Hong Kong Coliseum

Kowloon Park

TSIM SHA TSUI

Hong Kong Museum of History

7

Kowloon Mosque

6

The Royal Pacific Hotel & Towers

Canton Road

Hotel Omni Prince

Harbour City Cinema

Canton Hot Gossip

Omni Marco Polo Hotel

Ocean Centre

Kimberley

Kimberley Street

Miramar Hotel

Cameron Road

Granville Road

Hau Fook St

Park Hotel

Times Bookshop

International Hotel

Cameron Road

Grand Hotel

Guangdong Hotel

Prat Avenue

Ramada Inn Kowloon

Humphreys Avenue

China City Nightclub

Mody Road

Peninsula Centre

Royal Garden Hotel

Regal Meridien Road

Hotel Nikko

Shangri-La Hotel

Tsimshatsui Centre

Empire Centre

Holiday Inn Harbour View

Waterfront Promenade

Haiphong Road

Kowloon Park Drive

Ramada Renaissance Hotel

Peking Road

Swindon Books

Look Road

Harkow Road

Astor Hotel

Holiday Inn Golden Mile

Chungking Mansions

Imperial Hotel

Ambassador Hotel

Hyatt Regency

Kowloon Hotel

Hanoi Road

Mody Road

Chatham Road

Empress Hotel

Wing On Plaza

Mody Road

Hoverferry Pier (To Central)

Cross Harbour Tunnel

Omni The Hong Kong Hotel

Star House

Bus Terminus

2

Marine Police Headquarters

Middle Road

4 The Peninsula Hotel

Sheraton Hotel

Minden Row

5 Signal Hill Garden

Salisbury Road

Hong Kong Space Museum

1 Clock Tower

3 Hong Kong Cultural Centre

Star Ferry Pier (To Central/Wanchai)

Kowloon Pier

New World Centre

New World Hotel

Regent Hotel

Victoria Harbour

Legend

▬▬▬	KCR Route
- - - -	MTR Route
✳	MTR Station Entrances

0   100   200   300 m

0   100   200   300 yards

Kowloon Peninsula

© The Guidebook Company Ltd

Map 4

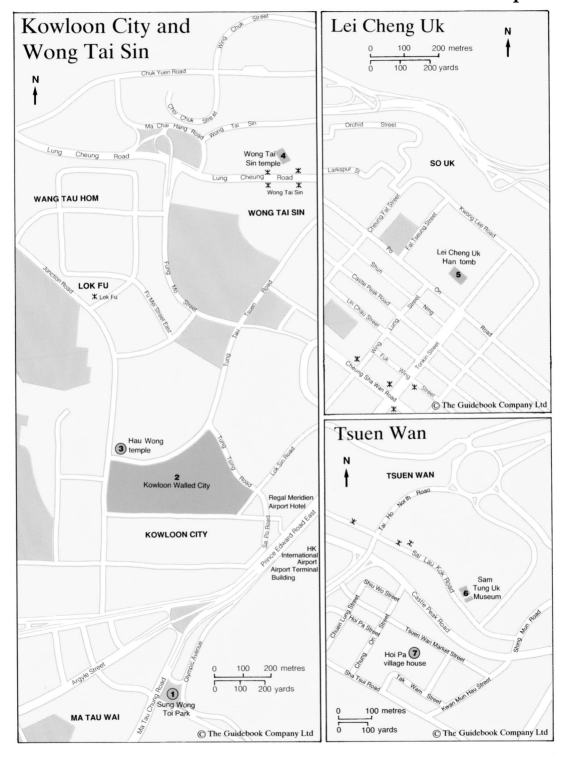

Kowloon City and Wong Tai Sin

N

Wing Chuk Street

Chuk Yuen Road

Choi Chuk Street

Ma Chai Hang Road   Wong Tai Sin

Lung Cheung Road

Wong Tai Sin temple **4**

Lung Cheung Road

Wong Tai Sin

WANG TAU HOM

WONG TAI SIN

Junction Road

Fung Mo Street

Fu Mei Street East

Tung Tau Tsuen Road

LOK FU

Lok Fu

Hau Wong **3** temple

2
Kowloon Walled City

Regal Meridien Airport Hotel

Sa Po Road

Prince Edward Road East

KOWLOON CITY

HK International Airport Airport Terminal Building

Lok Sin Road

Tung Tsing Road

Argyle Street

Ma Tau Chung Road

Olympic Avenue

0   100   200 metres
0   100   200 yards

1
Sung Wong Toi Park

MA TAU WAI

© The Guidebook Company Ltd

Lei Cheng Uk

N

0   100   200 metres
0   100   200 yards

Orchid Street

Larkspur St

SO UK

Cheung Fat Street

Fat Tseung Street

Kwong Lee Road

Po

Shun

Castle Peak Road

Un Chau Street

Lei Cheng Uk Han tomb **5**

On

Lung Street

Ning

Road

Wing Fuk Wing Street

Tonkin Street

Cheung Sha Wan Road

© The Guidebook Company Ltd

Tsuen Wan

N

TSUEN WAN

Tai Ho North Road

Sai Lau Kok Road

Shiu Wo Street

Chuen Lung Street

Hoi Pa Street

On Street

Castle Peak Road

Tsuen Wan Market Street

Sam Tung Uk Museum **6**

Shing Mun Road

Chung Street

Hoi Pa **7** village house

Sha Tsui Road

Tak Wan Street

Kwan Mun Hau Street

0   100 metres
0   100 yards

© The Guidebook Company Ltd

Map 5

Lantau Island

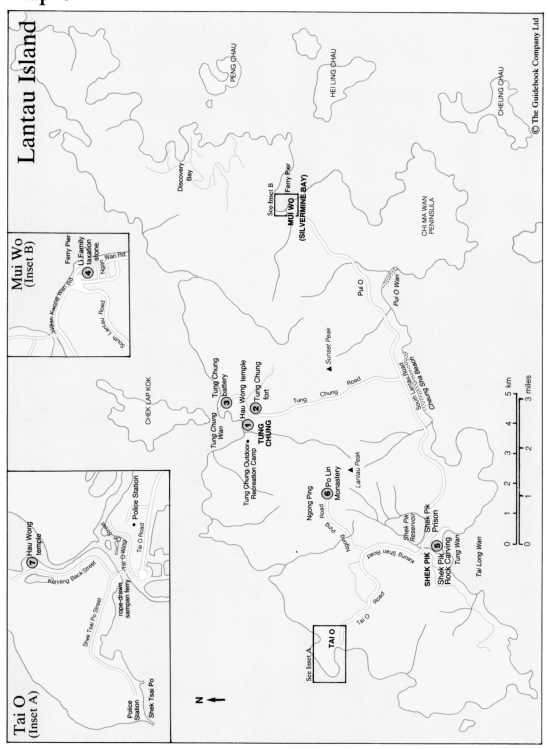

© The Guidebook Company Ltd

Tai O (Inset A)

- Hau Wong temple ⑦
- Police Station
- Tai O Road
- Kat Hing Back Street
- Tai O Wing On Street
- Shek Tsai Po Street
- rope-drawn sampan ferry
- Police Station
- Shek Tsai Po

Mui Wo (Inset B)

- Ferry Pier
- LI Family taxation stone ④
- South Lantau Road
- Ngan Kwong Wan Rd
- Ngan Wan Rd

PENG CHAU

HEI LING CHAU

CHEUNG CHAU

Discovery Bay

See Inset B

MUI WO (SILVERMINE BAY)

Ferry Pier

CHI MA WAN PENINSULA

Pui O

Pui O Wan

CHEK LAP KOK

Tung Chung battery ③

Hau Wong temple ①

TUNG CHUNG

Tung Chung fort ②

Tung Chung Wan

Tung Chung/Outdoor Recreation Camp

▲ Sunset Peak

Tung Chung Road

South Lantau Road

Cheung Sha Beach

Po Lin Monastery ⑥

▲ Lantau Peak

Ngong Ping Road

Shek Pik Reservoir

Keung Shan Road

Shek Pik Prison ⑤

SHEK PIK

Shek Pik Rock Carving

Tung Wan

Tai Long Wan

Ngong Ping Road

See Inset A

TAI O

Tai O Road

N

| 0 | 1 | 2 | 3 | 4 | 5 km |
| 0 | 1 | 2 | 3 miles |

Map 6

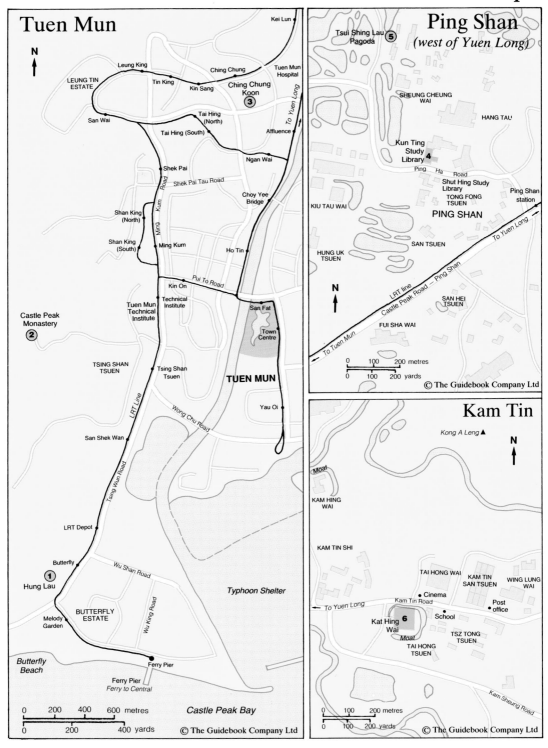

Tuen Mun

N

Kei Lun

Leung King

LEUNG TIN ESTATE

Tin King

Ching Chung

Tuen Mun Hospital

Kin Sang

Ching Chung Koon ③

San Wai

Tai Hing (North)

To Yuen Long

Tai Hing (South)

Affluence

Ngan Wai

Shek Pai

Shek Pai Tau Road

Choy Yee Bridge

Kum Road

Shan King (North)

Ming Road

Shan King (South)

Ming Kum

Ho Tin

Pui To Road

Kin On

Technical Institute

Tuen Mun Technical Institute

San Fat

Castle Peak Monastery ②

Town Centre

TSING SHAN TSUEN

Tsing Shan Tsuen

TUEN MUN

Yau Oi

LRT Line

Wong Chu Road

San Shek Wan

Tsing Wun Road

LRT Depot

Butterfly

Wu Shan Road

Hung Lau ①

Typhoon Shelter

Melody Garden

BUTTERFLY ESTATE

Wu King Road

Butterfly Beach

Ferry Pier

Ferry Pier
Ferry to Central

Castle Peak Bay

0   200   400   600 metres

0   200   400 yards

© The Guidebook Company Ltd

Ping Shan
(west of Yuen Long)

Tsui Shing Lau Pagoda ⑤

SHEUNG CHEUNG WAI

HANG TAU

Kun Ting Study Library ④

Ping   Ha   Road

Shut Hing Study Library

KIU TAU WAI

TONG FONG TSUEN

PING SHAN

Ping Shan station

SAN TSUEN

HUNG UK TSUEN

LRT line

Castle Peak Road – Ping Shan

To Yuen Long

SAN HEI TSUEN

N

FUI SHA WAI

To Tuen Mun

0   100   200 metres

0   100   200 yards

© The Guidebook Company Ltd

Kam Tin

Kong A Leng ▲

N

Moat

KAM HING WAI

KAM TIN SHI

TAI HONG WAI

KAM TIN SAN TSUEN

WING LUNG WAI

Cinema

Kam Tin Road

Post office

To Yuen Long

School

Kat Hing Wai ⑥

TSZ TONG TSUEN

Moat

TAI HONG TSUEN

Kam Sheung Road

0   100   200 metres

0   100   200 yards

© The Guidebook Company Ltd

Map 7

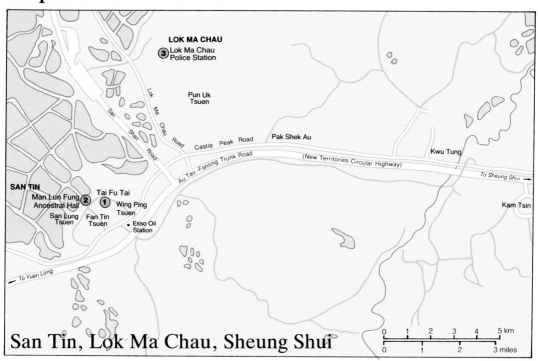

LOK MA CHAU

③ Lok Ma Chau
  Police Station

Pun Uk
Tsuen

Lok Ma Chau Road

San Shan Road

Castle Peak Road   Pak Shek Au

Au Tau-Fanling Trunk Road

(New Territories Circular Highway)   Kwu Tung

To Sheung Shui

SAN TIN

Man Lun Fung ② Tai Fu Tai
Ancestral Hall   ① Wing Ping
                      Tsuen
San Lung   Fan Tin
Tsuen   Tsuen
            • Esso Oil
              Station

Kam Tsin

← To Yuen Long

0	1	2	3	4	5 km
0	1		2		3 miles

San Tin, Lok Ma Chau, Sheung Shui

Sha Tin

Pai Tau Hang

Sha Tin Rural Committee Road   Sha Tin Wai Road

SHA TIN WAI

Lucky Plaza

3
Man Fat Tsz
10,000 Buddhas
Monastery

Pai Tau St.

Wang Pok Street
Sha Tin Centre
Tam Kon Po Street

Sha Tin
Town Hall

Yiu Wah St.

Pai Tau

Sha Tin
Station

New
Town
Plaza

Sha Tin
Park
Central

Shing Mun River Channel

Tai Chung Kiu Road

YUE
SHING
COURT

POK HONG
ESTATE

Tao Fong Shan   Tin Liu
Christian Centre
2

Magistracy
Royal
Park
Hotel

Sha Kok Street

Sha Tin Road

To Fung Shan Road

KCR line

Tai Po Road

Sha Tin

Pak Hok Ting St.

82M Bus
Stop

JAT MIN
TSUEN

Lai Chi
Yuen

Map 8

NT Regional
Headquarters

Government
Offices

Tung Lo
Wan

Man Lam Road

Bus Depot

Lion Rock Tunnel Road

1 Tsang Tai Uk
      (Shan Ha Wai)

0	100	200	300 metres
0	100	200	300 yards

Tung Lo Wan Hill Road

Tai Po Road

Tai Wai

Sing Chuen Road

Sing Wan Road

Mei Tin Road

Che Kung Miu Road

CHUN
SHEK
ESTATE

Fung Shek St.

FUNG
SHING
COURT

Che Kung
Temple

Shing Tin Street

Sha Tin Tau Rd.

N ↑

Map 7 (Cont.)

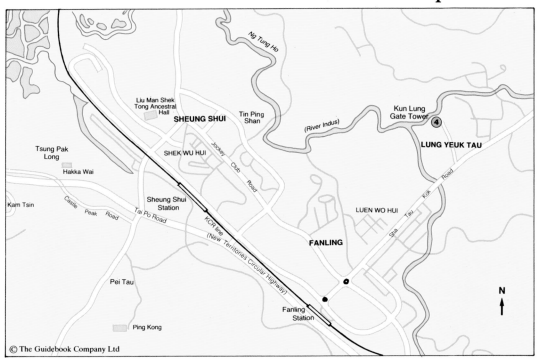

Ng Tung Ho

Liu Man Shek
Tong Ancestral
Hall

SHEUNG SHUI

Tin Ping
Shan

(River Indus)

Kun Lung
Gate Tower

④

LUNG YEUK TAU

Tsung Pak
Long

SHEK WU HUI

Jockey Club Road

Sha Tau Kok Road

Hakka Wai

Kam Tsin

Castle Peak Road

Sheung Shui
Station

Tai Po Road

KCR line
(New Territories Circular Highway)

LUEN WO HUI

FANLING

Pei Tau

Fanling
Station

N

Ping Kong

© The Guidebook Company Ltd

Map 9

Tai Po

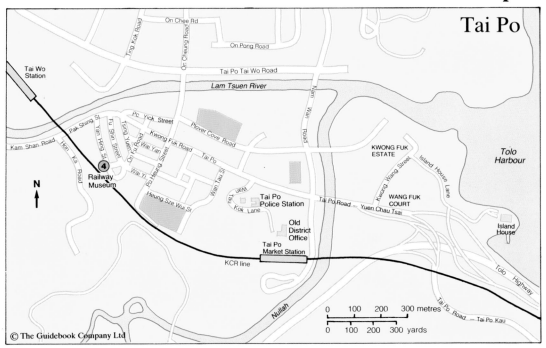

Ting Kok Road

On Chee Rd

On Cheung Road

On Pong Road

Tai Wo
Station

Tai Po Tai Wo Road

Lam Tsuen River

Nam Wan Road

Pak Shung St

Yan Hing St

Fu Shin Street

Tsing Yuen St

On Fu Road

Pc Yick Street

Kwong Fuk Road

Plover Cove Road

Kam Shan Road

Wai Yan St

Tai Po St

*Tolo
Harbour*

KWONG FUK
ESTATE

Island House Lane

Hon Ka Road

④

Railway
Museum

Po Heung Street

Wai Yi St

Heung Sze Wui St

Tai Tau St

Yuen

Kok Lane

Tai Po
Police Station

Tai Po Road Yuen Chau Tsai

Kwong Wang Street

WANG FUK
COURT

N

Old
District
Office

Island
House

Tai Po
Market Station

KCR line

Nullah

Tolo Highway

Tai Po Road Tai Po Kau

| 0 | 100 | 200 | 300 metres |
| 0 | 100 | 200 | 300 yards |

© The Guidebook Company Ltd

Map 10

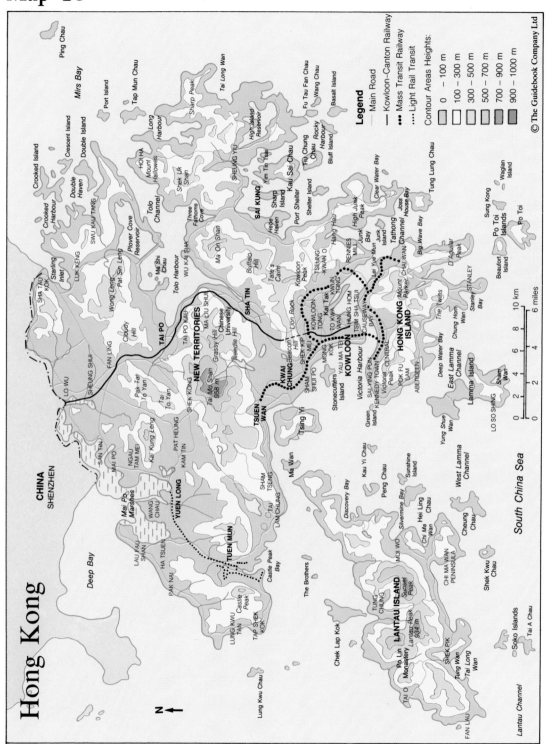

Hong Kong

Legend

— Main Road

‒‒‒ Kowloon-Canton Railway

••••• Mass Transit Railway

····· Light Rail Transit

Contour Areas Heights:

0 – 100 m
100 – 300 m
300 – 500 m
500 – 700 m
700 – 900 m
900 – 1000 m

© The Guidebook Company Ltd

N

10 km

6 miles

0   2   4   6   8

0   2   4   6

CHINA
SHENZHEN

NEW TERRITORIES

SAI KUNG

TAI PO

SHA TIN

TSUEN WAN

YUEN LONG

TUEN MUN

KWAI CHUNG

KOWLOON

HONG KONG ISLAND

LANTAU ISLAND

Mirs Bay

Deep Bay

South China Sea

Lantau Channel

Ping Chau

Crooked Island

Crescent Island

Double Island

Port Island

Tap Mun Chau

Tai Long Wan

Sharp Peak

Long Harbour

High Island Reservoir

Fu Tau Fan Chau

Wang Chau

Basalt Island

Tiu Chung Chau

Rocky Harbour

Bluff Island

Tung Lung Chau

Waglan Island

Po Toi

Sung Kong

Po Toi Islands

Beaufort Island

D'Aguilar Peak

STANLEY

Stanley Bay

Chung Hom

Deep Water Bay

Big Wave Bay

Clear Water Bay

Joss House Bay

Tathong Channel

Mount Parker

Junk Island

Junk Peak

High Junk Peak

Hang Hau

TSEUNG KWAN O

RENNIES MILL

Shelter Island

Port Shelter

Sharp Island

Hebe Haven

Yim Tin Tsai

Kau Sai Chau

SHEUNG YIU

HOI HA

Mount Hallowes

Shek Uk Shan

Tolo Channel

Three Fathoms Cove

Ma On Shan

Buffalo Hill

Tate's Cairn

Kowloon Peak

Lion Rock

KOWLOON TONG

Kai Tak

TO KWA WAN

HUNG HOM

TSIM SHA TSUI

YAU MA TEI

MONG KOK

SHAM SHUI PO

Victoria Harbour

KENNEDY TOWN

SAI YING PUN

CENTRAL

Victoria Peak

POK FU LAM

ABERDEEN

The Twins

STANLEY

Green Island

Stonecutters Island

Lei Yue Mun

CAUSEWAY BAY

KWUN TONG

Beacon Hill

SHEK KIP MEI

Needle Hill

Grassy Hill

Chinese University

MA LIU SHUI

TAI PO KAU

Wu Kai Sha

Ma Shi Chau

Tolo Harbour

Plover Cove Reservoir

Pat Sin Leng

Wong Leng

SWU KAU TANG

Starling Inlet

SHA TAU KOK

LUK KENG

Crooked Harbour

Double Haven

Crooked Island

Crooked Harbour

FAN LING

SHEUNG SHUI

LO WU

LO U

SAN TIN

MAI PO

Mai Po Marshes

LAU FAU SHAN

HA TSUEN

PAK NAI

Deep Bay

Lung Kwu Chau

LUNG KWU TAN

TAP SHEK KOK

Castle Peak

Castle Peak Bay

The Brothers

Chek Lap Kok

Lantau Peak 934 m

Sunset Peak

TUNG CHUNG

TAI O

Po Lin Monastery

SHEK PIK

Tai Long Wan

Tung Wan

FAN LAU

Tai A Chau

Soko Islands

Shek Kwu Chau

CHI MA WAN PENINSULA

Cheung Chau

Chi Ma Wan

Hei Ling Chau

Silvermine Bay

MUI WO

Discovery Bay

Peng Chau

Kau Yi Chau

Sunshine Island

Ma Wan

Tsing Yi

Yung Shue Wan

Lamma Island

West Lamma Channel

East Lamma Channel

LO SO SHING

Sham Wan

PAT HEUNG

KAM TIN

SHAM TSENG

TAI CHUNG

LAM CHUNG

WANG CHAU

NGAU TAM MEI

Kai Kung Leng

Tai To Yan

Pak Tai To Yan

Cloudy Hill

SHEK KONG

Tai Mo Shan 958 m

Tsz Ma Tei

TABLE OF CHINESE DYNASTIES

Shang Dynasty	*c* 1550 -	*c* 1030 BC
Zhou Dynasty	*c* 1030 -	*c* 256
Qin Dynasty	221 -	207
Han Dynasty	202 BC -	AD 220
Three Kingdoms Dynasty	221 -	265
Six Dynasties	265 -	581
Sui Dynasty	581 -	618
Tang Dynasty	618 -	906
Five Dynasties	907 -	960
Song Dynasty	960 -	1279
Yuan Dynasty	1260 -	1368
Ming Dynasty	1368 -	1644
Qing Dynasty	1644 -	1912

SIGNIFICANT HONG KONG DATES

Formation of Hong Kong's present coastline	5th millennium BC
Stone Age	5th millennium - 1200 BC
Bronze Age	1200 BC
Yueh people conquered by the Qin	214 BC
Hong Kong incorporated into the Han Empire	111 BC
Song boy emperors based in the Hong Kong region	AD 1275 - 1279
Hong Kong claimed as a British Colony	1841
Treaty of Nanking *(cession of Hong Kong Island to the United Kingdom)*	1843
Convention of Peking *(cession of the Kowloon Peninsula to the United Kingdom)*	1860
Convention of Peking *(cession of the New Territories to the United Kingdom)*	1898
Fall of Hong Kong to the Japanese	1941
End of the Japanese occupation and return to British rule	1945
Hong Kong will become a Special Administrative Region of the People's Republic of China	1997

DERIVATION OF HONG KONG PLACE NAMES

Aberdeen	Lord Aberdeen (British Foreign Secretary 1841 – 6)
Albert Path	Prince Albert (husband of Queen Victoria)
Aldrich Bay/Street	Major Aldrich (Royal Engineers)
Anton Street	C E Anton (Jardine, Matheson & Co)
Babington Path	Anthony Babington (Shewan, Tomes and Co)
Barker Road	Major General Digby Barker
Belcher's Street	Captain Sir Edward Belcher (*HMS Sulphur*)
Bisney Road	Dhunjibhoy Bisney (Indian merchant)
Black's Link	Major General Wilsone Black (GOC Hong Kong)
Blake's Pier	Sir Henry Blake (Governor 1898 – 1903)
Bonham Road	Sir Samuel Bonham (Governor 1848 – 54)
Bowen Road	Sir George Bowen (Governor 1883 – 85)
Bowring Street	Sir John Bowring (Governor 1854 – 59)
Boyce Road	Edward Boyce (Director of Public Works 1949 – 50)
Braga Circuit	Jose Pedro Braga (Legislative Councillor)
Brewin Path	A W Brewin (Registrar General 1901)
Bridges Street	Dr W T Bridges (Acting Attorney General and Acting Colonial Secretary)
Bulkeley Street	Francis Bulkeley Johnson (Jardine, Matheson & Co)
Burd Street	John Burd (Merchant)
Caine Road	Colonel William Caine (Hong Kong's first Chief

	Magistrate, later Colonial Secretary)
Caldecott Road	Sir Andrew Caldecott (Governor 1935 – 37)
Cameron Road	Major General W G Cameron
Cape Collinson	Lieutenant Collinson, RE (Surveyor)
Cape D'Aguilar	Major General D'Aguilar (Hong Kong's first Lieutenant Governor)
Catchick Street	Sir Paul Catchick Chater
Chater Road	Sir Paul Chater (Legislative Councillor)
Cheung Po Tsai Cave	Cheung Po Tsai (Pirate Chief)
Clarendon Street	Lord Clarendon (Foreign Secretary 1853 – 58)
Cleverly Street	Charles St G Cleverly (Acting Surveyor General 1845 – 65)
Cochrane Street	Admiral Sir Thomas Cochrane
Connaught Road	Duke of Connaught
Cooper Road	Francis Cooper (Director of Public Works 1891 – 97)
Creasy Road	Harold Creasy (Director of Public Works 1923 – 32)
Derby Road	Lord Derby (Secretary of State for the Colonies 1882 – 91)
Des Voeux Road	Sir William Des Voeux (Governor 1887 – 91)
Dodwell's Ridge	George Dodwell (The Dock Company)
Duddell Street	George Duddell (Merchant)
Dyer Avenue	Robert Dyer (The Dock Company)
Elgin Street	Lord Elgin (Envoy Extraordinary to China)
Elliot Crescent	Captain Charles Elliot (Royal Navy)
Fleming Road	F Fleming (Colonial Secretary)

Gascoigne Road	Major General W J Gascoigne
Granville Road	Earl Granville (Secretary of State for the Colonies 1868 – 70)
Gresson Street	W J Gresson (Jardine, Matheson & Co)
Gutzlaff Street	Rev C Gutzlaff (Chinese Secretary 1840)
Harcourt Road	Rear Admiral Sir Cecil Harcourt
Hart Avenue	Sir Robert Hart (Inspector General, Chinese Maritime Customs Service)
Hatton Road	Major General V Hatton
Heard Street	George Heard (Union Dock Company)
Hebe Haven	*Young Hebe* survey vessel
Henderson Road	Richard Henderson (Director of Public Works)
Hennessy Road	Sir John Pope Hennessy (Governor 1877 – 82)
Hillier Street	C B Hillier (Chief Magistrate)
Hiram's Highway	Captain Hiram C Potts (Royal Marines)
Hollywood Road	Named after Sir John Davis' home, Hollywood Towers in England
Hysan Avenue	Lee Hysan (Entrepreneur)
Ice House Street	Site of first ice house
Irving Street	E A Irving (Inspector of Schools)
Jackson Road	Sir Thomas Jackson (Hong Kong & Shanghai Bank)
Jardine's Lookout/ Bazaar	William Jardine (Jardine, Matheson & Co)
Jervois Street	Major General Jervois (Lieutenant Governor 1852 –53)
Johnston Road	Sir Reginald Johnston (Commissioner for Weihaiwei)
Jordan Road/Valley	Sir John Jordan (British Minister in Peking)

Kadoorie Avenue	Sir Ellis Kadoorie (Merchant)
Kai Tak Airport	Sir Kai Ho Kai (Legislative Councillor) and Au Tak
Kellett Island	Sir Henry Kellett (Royal Navy)
Kennedy Town/Road	Sir Arthur Kennedy (Governor 1872 – 77)
Keswick Street	William Keswick (Jardine, Matheson & Co)
Kimberley Road	Earl of Kimberley (Secretary of State for the Colonies 1870 – 74)
King's Park	Named after Edward VII on his accession to the British throne in 1901
Knutsford Terrace	Lord Knutsford (Secretary of State for the Colonies 1887 – 92)
Kotewall Road	Robert Kotewall (Legislative Councillor)
Lady Clementi's Ride	Wife of Sir Cecil Clementi (Governor 1925 – 30)
Landale Street	David Landale (Jardine, Matheson & Co)
Lee Gardens	Lee Hysan (Entrepreneur)
Leighton Hill	F Leighton (Merchant)
Lockhart Road	Sir James Stewart Lockhart (Colonial Secretary)
Lower Albert Road	Prince Albert (husband of Queen Victoria)
Lower Lascar Row	Lascars were Muslim sailors from the Southern Philippines
Lugard Road	Sir Frederick Lugard (Governor 1907 – 12)
Lyndhurst Terrace	Lord Lyndhurst (British Lord Chancellor)
Macdonnell Road	Sir Richard Macdonnell (Governor 1866 – 72)
Marsh Road	W H Marsh (Colonial Secretary)
Matheson Street	James Matheson (Jardine, Matheson & Co)

May Road	Sir Henry May (Governor 1912 – 19)
Mercer Street	W T Mercer (Colonial Secretary)
Mody Road	Sir Hormusjee Mody (Parsee Merchant)
Mongkok	Erroneous romanisation of 'Wongkok'
Moorsom Road	Lewis Moorsom (Surveyor General 1868 – 73)
Morrison Hill	Robert Morrison (First Chinese Secretary)
Mount Austin Road	J Gardiner Austin (Colonial Secretary 1868 – 78)
Mount Davis	Sir John Davis (Governor 1844 – 48)
Mount Gough	Sir Hugh Gough (Lieutenant General)
Mount Johnston	A R Johnston (Colonial Secretary)
Mount Parker	Admiral Sir William Parker (Commander-in-chief)
Mount Stenhouse	Commodore Sir Humphrey Le Fleming Stenhouse
Murray Road	Sir George Murray (Secretary of State for the Colonies 1828 – 30)
Nathan Road	Sir Matthew Nathan (Governor 1904 – 07)
Northcote Close	Sir Geoffrey Northcote (Governor 1937 – 40)
Ormsby Street	Robert Ormsby (Director of Public Works 1897 – 1901)
Parkes Street	Sir Henry Parkes (British Consul at Canton)
Paterson Street	William Paterson (Jardine, Matheson & Co)
Pedder Street	Lieutenant William Pedder (Royal Navy, Hong Kong's first Harbour Master)
Peel Street	Sir Robert Peel (British Prime Minister)

Plover Cove	*HMS Plover*
Pound Lane	Former site of Government animal pound
Possession Street	Near Possession Point where Captain Elliot first landed on Hong Kong Island
Pottinger Street	Sir Henry Pottinger (Governor 1841 – 44)
Prince Edward Road	Prince Edward
Princess Margaret Road	Princess Margaret
Queen's Road	Queen Victoria
Rednaxela Terrace	Misspelt reversal of 'Alexandra', commemorating Queen Alexandra
Rennie's Mill	W H Rennie
Repulse Bay	*HMS Repulse*
Robinson Road	Sir Hercules Robinson (Governor)
Salisbury Road	Lord Salisbury (British Prime Minister 1885 – 86)
Sassoon Road	Albert Sassoon
Seymour Road	Sir Michael Seymour (Rear Admiral)
Sharp Peak/Island	Granville Sharp (Financier)
Shelley Street	A E Shelley (Auditor General)
Shouson Hill	Sir Shouson Chow
Stanley Street/Village	Lord Stanley (Secretary of State for the Colonies)
Staunton Street	Sir George Staunton
Stubbs Road	Sir Reginald Stubbs (Governor 1919 – 25)
Sulphur Channel	*HMS Sulphur*
Tonnochy Road	M S Tonnochy (Superintendent of the gaol)
Route Twisk	Acronym for Tsuen Wan to Sek Kong
Victoria	Queen Victoria
Wellington Street	Duke of Wellington

BIBLIOGRAPHY

Angus, Marjorie Bird, *Bamboo Connection*, Heinemann
Frank Cass, London, 1968.

Baker, Hugh D R, *Sheung Shui: A Chinese Lineage Village,*
Frank Cass, London, 1968.

Baker, Hugh, *Ancestral Images*, South China Morning Post,
Hong Kong, 1979.

Bard, Solomon, *In Search of the Past: A Guide to the
Antiquities of Hong Kong*, Urban Council, Hong Kong,
1988.

Birch, Alan and Cole, Martin, *Captive Years*, Heinemann
Asia, Hong Kong, 1982.

Bloomfield, Frena, *Scandals and Disasters of Hong Kong,*
South China Morning Post, Hong Kong, 1985.

Bonavia, David, *Hong Kong 1997*, South China Morning
Post, Hong Kong, 1983.

Bruce, Phillip, *Military History Notes, 1-6*, privately published
in Hong Kong, 1987.

Burkhardt, V R, *Chinese Creeds and Customs, Vols 1, 2 and 3.*

Cameron, Nigel, *Hong Kong: The Cultured Pearl*, Oxford
University Press, Hong Kong, 1978.

Cameron, Nigel, *The Milky Way: The History of Dairy Farm,*
The Dairy Farm Co. Ltd, Hong Kong, 1986.

Cha, Louis, *On Hong Kong's Future*, Ming Pao Daily News
Ltd, Hong Kong, 1984.

Chang, Kwang-chih, *The Archaeology of Ancient China,*
Fourth edition, Yale University Press, New Haven and
London, 1986.

Chung Wah Nan, *Contemporary Architecture in Hong Kong,*
Joint Publishing Company, Hong Kong, 1989.

Coates, Austin, *Prelude to Hong Kong*, Routledge and Kegan
Paul, London, 1966.

Coates, Austin, *A Macau Narrative*, Heinemann, Hong Kong,
1978.

Coates, Austin, *Whampoa: Ships on the Shore*, South China
Morning Post, 1980.

Collis, Maurice, *Foreign Mud*, Faber and Faber, London
1946.

Collis, Maurice, *Wayfoong*, Faber and Faber, London, 1965.

Cooper, John, *Colony in Conflict*, Swindon Book Company,
Hong Kong, 1970.

Eitel, E J, *Europe in China*, Oxford University Press, Hong Kong, 1983.

Endacott, G B, *A History of Hong Kong*, Oxford University Press, Hong Kong, 1958.

Endacott, G B, *Hong Kong Eclipse*, Oxford University Press, Hong Kong, 1978.

Faure, David, *The Structure of Chinese Rural Society: Lineage and Village in the Eastern New Territories, Hong Kong*, Oxford University Press, Hong Kong, 1986.

Faure, David, Hayes, James and Birch, Alan (Eds) *From Village to City*, University of Hong Kong, Hong Kong, 1984.

Finn, Daniel J, *Archaeological Finds on Lamma Island Near Hong Kong*, Ricci Publications, Hong Kong, 1958.

Freedman, Maurice, *Lineage Organization in Southeastern China*, The Athlone Press, London, 1958.

Gillingham, Paul, *At the Peak*, Macmillan, Hong Kong, 1983.

Graca, Jorge, *Fortifications of Macau*, Direccao dos Servicos de Turismo de Macau, Macau, 1984.

Harland, Kathleen, *The Royal Navy in Hong Kong since 1841*, Maritime Books, Liskeard, Cornwall, 1985.

Harris, Peter, *Hong Kong: A Study in Bureaucratic Politics*, Heinemann Asia, Hong Kong, 1978.

Harris, Peter, *Public Administration and Public Affairs in Hong Kong*, Heinemann Asia, 1983.

Hayes, James, *The Rural Communities of Hong Kong*, Oxford University Press, Hong Kong, 1983.

Hellman, Lilian (Ed) *The Selected Letters of Anton Chekhov*, Picador, London, 1984.

Hong Kong Government Information Services, *Hong Kong Heritage*, 1989.

Hong Kong Government Information Services, *Rural Architecture in Hong Kong*, 1979.

Hook, Brian (Ed) *The Cambridge Encyclopaedia of China*, Cambridge University Press, Cambridge, 1982.

Hughes, Richard, *Hong Kong: Borrowed Place – Borrowed Time*, André Deutsch, London, 1968.

Jao, Y C *et al* (Eds), *Hong Kong and 1997*, University of Hong Kong, Hong Kong, 1985.

Jarvie, I C (Ed), *Hong Kong: A Society in Transition*, Routledge and Kegan Paul, London, 1959.

Keightley, David (Ed) *The Origins of Chinese Civilization*,

University of California Press, Berkeley, 1963.

Keswick, Maggie, *The Thistle and the Jade*, Octopus Books, London, 1982.

Kong Kai Ming, *Paintings of Hong Kong Historic Landmarks*, Hong Kong Baptist College, Hong Kong, 1989.

Lawrence, Anthony, *The Taipan Traders*, Formasia, Hong Kong.

Leventhal, Dennis A. *The Jewish Community of Hong Kong*, The Jewish Historical Society of Hong Kong, 1986.

Luo, Xianglin, *Hong Kong and Its External Communications before 1842*, Institute of Chinese Culture, Hong Kong, 1963.

Mattock, Katherine, *The Story of Government House*, Government Information Services, Hong Kong, 1978.

McGurn, William, *Basic Law, Basic Questions*, Review Publishing Company, Hong Kong, 1988.

Meacham, William, *Rock Carvings in Hong Kong*, The Christian Study Centre, Hong Kong, 1976.

Meacham, William (Ed) *Sham Wan, Lamma Island — An Archaeological Site Study*, Journal Monograph III of the Hong Kong Archaeological Society, Hong Kong, 1978.

Meacham, William, *Archaeology in Hong Kong*, Heinemann, Hong Kong, 1980.

Miners, Norman, *The Government and Politics of Hong Kong*, Oxford University Press, 1975.

Miners, Norman, *Hong Kong Under Imperial Rule 1912–1941*, Oxford University Press, 1987.

Moores, Alan (Ed), *Another Hong Kong: an Explorer's Guide*, Emphasis, Hong Kong, 1989.

Morris, Jan, *Hong Kong: Epilogue to an Empire*, Viking, London, 1988.

Ng, Peter Y L, *New Peace County*, Hong Kong University Press, Hong Kong, 1983.

Pope-Hennessy, James, *Half-Crown Colony*, Jonathan Cape, London, 1969.

Rafferty, Kevin, *City on the Rocks*, Viking, London, 1989.

Rawson, Jessica, *Ancient China: Art and Archaeology*, British Museum, London, 1980.

Rodwell, Simon, *Boxes and Barnacles: The Story of Hong Kong International Terminals*, Hong Kong International Terminals, Hong Kong, 1989.

Rogers, Pamela Rumball and Ward, Valerie, *Stone Adzes of Hong Kong*, Urban Council, Hong Kong, 1987.

Savidge, Joyce, *This is Hong Kong: Temples*, Hong Kong Government, Hong Kong, 1977.

Sayer, G R, *Hong Kong 1841–1862*, Hong Kong University Press, Hong Kong, 1937.

Sayer, G R, *Hong Kong 1862–1919*, Hong Kong University Press, Hong Kong, 1975.

Schofield, W, *An Archaeological Site at Shek Pik*, Journal Monograph I, Hong Kong Archaeological Society, Hong Kong, 1975.

Sinclair, Kevin, *Asia's Finest*, Unicorn, Hong Kong, 1983.

Sinn, Elizabeth, *Power and Charity*, Hong Kong University Press, Hong Kong, 1900.

Stevens-Smith, Joyce, *Matilda*, Matilda and War Memorial Hospital, Hong Kong, 1988.

Tang, M, Dunning, I, Baker, A H, Martin, E M, *Historical Hong Kong Walks Hong Kong Island*, The Guidebook Company, Hong Kong, 1988.

Vaid, K N, *The Overseas Indian Community*, Hong Kong University Press, Hong Kong, 1972.

Walden, John, *Excellency, Your Gap is Growing*, All Noble Company, Hong Kong, 1987.

Watt, J C Y, *A Han Tomb in Lei Cheng Uk*, Urban Council, Hong Kong, 1983.

Wesley-Smith, Peter, *Unequal Treaty 1898–1997*, Oxford University Press, Hong Kong, 1980.

Wesley-Smith, Peter and Chen, Albert (Eds), *The Basic Law and Hong Kong's Future*, Butterworths, Hong Kong, 1988.

Whyte, Robert Orr (Ed), *The Evolution of the East Asian Environment*, University of Hong Kong, Hong Kong, 1984.

Yip, C H, *History Around Us*, Urban Council, Hong Kong, 1982.

Young, Gavin, *Beyond the Lion Rock*, Hutchinson, London, 1988.

INDEX

MIS/37/02